Harvard Works Because We Do

Harvard Works Because We Do

PHOTOGRAPHS AND INTERVIEWS BY GREG HALPERN · FOREWORD BY STUDS TERKEL

THE QUANTUCK LANE PRESS
NEW YORK

Yanick Dunwell, Server, Private Catering Service

Return of Organization Exempt From Income Tax

Under section 501(c) of the Internal Revenue Code (except black lung benefit trust or private foundation) or section 4947(a)(1) nonexempt charitable trust

OMB No 1545-0047

1999

This Form is Open to Public Inspection

Department of the Treasury
Internal Revenue Service

Note The organization may have to use a copy of this return to satisfy state reporting requirements

A For the 1999 calendar year, OR tax year period beginning **July 1** , 1999, and ending **June 30, 2000**

B Check if:
- [X] Change of address
- [ ] Initial return
- [ ] Final return
- [ ] Amended return (required also for State reporting)

C Name of organization
President and Fellows of Harvard College

Number and street (or P O box if mail is not delivered to street address)
1350 Massachusetts Avenue

Room/suite
Room 481

City or town
Cambridge

State or Country
MA

ZIP code
02138

D Employer identification number
04-2103580

E Telephone number
(617) 496-0299

F Check [ ] if exemption application is pending

G Type of organization [X] Exempt under section 501(c)(**3**)(insert no.) [ ] section 4947(a)(1) nonexempt charitable trust

Note Section 501(c)(3) exempt organizations and 4947(a)(1) nonexempt charitable trusts MUST attach a completed Sch A (Form 990)

H(a) Is this a group return filed for affiliates? Yes or No   **No**

I If either box in H is checked "Yes," enter four-digit group exemption number (GEN)

(b) If "Yes," enter the number of affiliates for which this return is filed   **0**

(c) Is this a separate return filed by an organization covered by a group ruling?   **No**

J Accounting method: [ ] Cash [X] Accrual [ ] Other (specify)

K Check here [ ] if the organization's gross receipts are normally not more than $25,000. The organization need not file a return with the IRS, but if it received a Form 990 Package in the mail, it should file a return without financial data Some states require a complete return

Note Form 990-EZ may be used by organizations with gross receipts less than $100,000 and total assets less than $250,000 at end of year

Part I Revenue, Expenses, and Changes in Net Assets or Fund Balances   (See Specific Instructions on page 15.)

1	Contributions, gifts, grants, and similar amounts received:		
a	Direct public support	1a	565,488,027
b	Indirect public support	1b	0
c	Government contributions (grants)	1c	327,184,382
d	Total (add lines 1a through 1c) (attach schedule of contributors) (cash $ 767,382,633 noncash $ 125,289,775)	1d	892,672,408
2	Program service revenue including government fees and contracts (from Part VII, line 93)	2	772,788,242
3	Membership dues and assessments	3	1,395,938
4	Interest on savings and temporary cash investments	4	0
5	Dividends and interest from securities	5	340,082,797
6a	Gross rents	6a	39,289,353
b	Less: rental expenses	6b	(30,293,798)
c	Net rental income or (loss) (subtract line 6b from line 6a)	6c	8,995,555
7	Other investment income (describe)	7	0

8a Gross amount from sales of assets other than inventory	(A) Securities	(B) Other		
	3,929,762,547 8a	1,839,500		
b Less: cost or other basis and sales expenses	0 8b	(382,452)		
c Gain or (loss) (attach schedule)	3,929,762,547 8c	1,457,048		

d	Net gain or (loss) (combine line 8c, columns (A) and (B))	8d	3,931,219,595
9	Special events and activities (attach schedule)		
a	Gross revenue (not including $ of contributions reported on line 1a)	9a	
b	Less: direct expenses other than fundraising expenses	9b	
c	Net income or (loss) from special events (subtract line 9b from line 9a)	9c	0
10a	Gross sales of inventory, less returns and allowances	10a	
b	Less: cost of goods sold	10b	
c	Gross profit or (loss) from sales of inventory (attach schedule) (subtract line 10b from line 10a)	10c	0
11	Other revenue (from Part VII, line 103)	11	20,001,769
12	Total revenue (add lines 1d, 2, 3, 4, 5, 6c, 7, 8d, 9c, 10c, and 11)	12	5,967,156,304
13	Program services (from line 44, column (B))	13	1,792,510,854
14	Management and general (from line 44, column (C))	14	103,903,702
15	Fundraising (from line 44, column (D))	15	53,720,344
16	Payments to affiliates (attach schedule)	16	0
17	Total expenses (add lines 16 and 44, column (A))	17	1,950,134,900
18	Excess or (deficit) for the year (subtract line 17 from line 12)	18	4,017,021,404
19	Net assets or fund balances at beginning of year (from line 73, column (A))	19	17,598,909,000
20	Other changes in net assets or fund balances (attach explanation)	20	1,036,973,000
21	Net assets or fund balances at end of year (combine lines 18, 19, and 20)	21	22,652,903,404

For Paperwork Reduction Act Notice, see page 1 of the separate instructions.   (HTA)   Form 990 (1999)

Ex-pen-ses

Net Assets

Foreword

Studs Terkel

Greg Halpern has put forth one of the most hopeful and exhilarating books in recent years. He has captured the custodians of Harvard in photographs as indelible as the words of his unsung heroes. "Custodians" is an all-encompassing word for the hitherto face-less workingmen and -women—the janitors, the cleaning ladies, the waitresses, the chefs, the security guards, the truck handlers—who have served the faculty, the students, and the administration of the most richly endowed educational institution in the world.

The administration of Harvard had not given much thought to those who guarded the doors, changed the lightbulbs, made the beds, and mopped the floors of halls bearing Brahmin names. Theirs is not a share-the-wealth program, i.e., offering a living wage to those "others" who, like well-behaved children, were to be seen but not heard. And the trade unions, through the past several years, had not had much luck with the administration. But it was a motley group of these kids, the few students usually called starry-eyed idealists—or trouble-makers, for that matter—who in their sit-in at the administration building set off a bonfire for equity and justice. It was the testimonies—distributed as photocopies, read at rallies, and now printed in this book—that had inspired them.

For the students who sat-in, the odds at first were overwhelmingly against them. Yet something remarkable and wholly unexpected happened. Other students, who might otherwise have been interested only in making it postgraduately big, gathered around. Faculty members, who might not have taught Ethics 101 but who did practice it, joined the young sitters-in in protest. The press saw an honest-to-God story here and let the rest of society know about it and, of course, the custodians, on whose behalf it was, were exhilarated and suddenly rich with hope.

The administration, which until this moment said "Never"—the president had vowed to resign rather than negotiate—finally bowed. Considerable concessions were won. There was a celebratory victory: truly a heroic one. Most important, it was an unprecedented one. The students and the blue collars had together triumphed. During the tumultuous and stirring sixties, campus kids all around the country had participated in the civil rights and anti–Vietnam War movements. But they were distant from the blue collars and, for that matter, it was the other way around, too. There was an unfortunate gap between them. What happened in Seattle was the first sign that times were a-changin'. And it was the Harvard University sit-in that was the climactic moment.

Greg Halpern was one of those fifty sitters-in. Fortunately and fortuitously, he is a remarkable chronicler, as an interviewer as well as a photographer. He has caught the words—the visions, the dreams, the hopes—of these "others," and this book is yet another chance to share them with people who otherwise might never have seen them.

The custodians of Harvard now have faces and voices and they are eloquent, natural-born storytellers. From Carol-Ann Malatesta, as she bends over, wringing out the mop: "The work itself sucks, all right? It's very tiring, and it's hard work, especially if one of the kids pukes. The kids drink, and they puke, and it dries on the walls and that's kind of gross. But you just clean it up, you hold your nose and you think to yourself, 'I got three kids, I love my kids, I love my kids. I want the kids to be happy. The kids are going get to college! And they're going get pregnant by someone with a degree and a job, not like their mother!' " Beat that, if you can.

The photographs are all lollapaloozas. One of the final pictures says it all. The university president Larry Summers is holding forth at a conference as Jean Phane, a custodian, across the table, studiously observes him (p. 146). We see one member of our species enthralled by another, vastly distant though somewhat curious, fellow human. It knocked me out. So does the rest of this book.

CREACIONES SUPLIMARVER

BRAGAS · GUANTES · BOTAS Y EQUIPOS
DE SEGURIDAD INDUSTRIAL

Apellidos: DAZA PULGARIN

Nombres: MARTA LUCIDIA
PRESIDENTE

C. I. No. V· 15319631

Mirtha L. Daza P.
FIRMA AUTORIZADA

UNICCÓ

Lotus.

WHITE GLOVE CLEANING CO.

Name

Daza, Marta L.

034-78-7589

McGARR SERVICE CORP.

Name

Daza, Marta L.

034-78-7589

CSC Consolidated Service Corporation

Marta L. Daza
Name

Marta L Daza

034-78-7589
Social Security Number

2614
Employee Number

MARTA DAZA

CLEANER
2368001

03/10/99 WENTWORTH
INSTITUTE

Marta L Daza

UNICCO

HARVARD
UNIVERSIT
SPECIAL

Longwood Area
Vendor
WHITE GLOVE

MARTA DAZA
012 02358 1

VALID THRU· 12/31/00
FOR IDENTIFICATION ONLY

Alfred Eric Alden

Born on: April 27, 1977. Secondary School: Pin
School. Home Address: 1528 Middle River Dri
Lauderdale, FL 33304. Field of Concentration: F
Harvard College Scholarship. Signet Society.
Activities: House Committee (Chair).

Frank Edward Pacheco

Born on: October 13, 1977. Secondary School:
School. Home Address: 453 Fifth Street, Brookl
11215. Field of Concentration: Economics and F
Harvard College Scholarship. Harvard Asso
Cultivating Inter-American Democracy (Admini
Director). Model Congress. Tiddlywinks
(Chancellor). House Activities: House Committee (

Gregory Ross Halpern

Born on: August 4, 1977. Secondary School: City
High School. Home Address: 256 Woodbridge A
Buffalo, NY 14214. Field of Concentration: Hist
Literature. Harvard College Scholarship. Firs
Outdoor Program Leader (Steering Committee).

Introduction

When I asked Gary Newmark—the first person I interviewed for this book—if I could talk to him about his job, his response was, "You want to know about regular working stiffs? You want to know what I do? I unloaded from a truck probably every book you ever read at Harvard. That's what I do." It was my first honest conversation with a campus service worker.

There is a deliberate aura of wealth and power at Harvard, and it is tended to by more than a thousand workers. They dust the portraits, polish the oak panels, and prune the trees. They cook the food and guard the campus; they work in every room of every building, day and night, and yet one of their frequent complaints is that the nation's most perceptive students and scholars simply do not see them.

I was embarrassed when someone had to explain to me that the reason the lights were on all night in Harvard's buildings was because crews of custodians were in those buildings, working all night to clean up the mess of the day before. Then, during my junior year I read Studs Terkel's *Working,* and I was shocked no teacher had ever assigned me that book or any other workers' histories, for that matter. Later that year, I went to a meeting my childhood friend Aaron Bartley had called about starting a living wage campaign on campus. At the meeting, I learned that while Harvard had recently broken all records for university fund raising—the endowment had nearly tripled from $7 billion to $20 billion between 1994 and 2001—the university had, at the same time, been cutting the wages and benefits of its lowest-paid employees through outsourcing (contracting to private firms). Amazed, I presented an outline of what would become this book to the History and Literature department as my proposed senior thesis topic. It was rejected, on the grounds that it was not adequately academically rigorous. The rejection only made me more stubborn. I started the project anyway, and after graduating I spent the next three years working on it.

Personally, I was comfortable as an undergraduate, but I always worked. I inspected bags in a library, I tended to a research greenhouse, I cleaned student dorm rooms and bathrooms, I shelved books in Widener Library, and after graduating, I worked as a carpenter's assistant on campus. At one point, during my stint as a carpenter, my supervisor had assigned me the uncommonly monotonous task of drilling countless tiny holes through a number of metal pieces. After a few hours of drilling, just before lunchtime, he walked up to me and gave me a hard look. "Twenty-three years old and sittin' at a drill press," he said. He shook his head in pity. "When I was your age I owned my own business."

Presumably, I was working as a carpenter's assistant not just to pay my bills but to learn something about class on campus, to inform this book. But after three years I often wondered why I was still hell-bent on making this book. It took me some time to recognize that my motivation was not only to tell workers' stories, but to try to understand my own as well. My grandfather had made the trip into the United States hidden in the bottom of an ocean liner. He spoke no English when he got to New York, and he found a job washing dishes. With time and luck, he would find a union job cutting glass, though he had to support two children and a wife. My father grew up very poor and he never forgot it. And he'll never let me forget it, perhaps because he did not fully identify with the solidly upper-middle-class community he found himself a part of later in life; he had become a professor, my mother a lawyer. Despite my own relative privilege and for reasons I still do not entirely understand, I have always felt a fierce alliance with my father's and grandfather's experiences. Perhaps because of that, I was never entirely comfortable at Harvard. On weekend nights, "Harvard men" would walk confidently around campus in tuxedoes, half drunk and singing a cappella. For a while, I tried to join in. I bought a tuxedo and joined the Phoenix, a wood-paneled, all-male social club. Primarily we drank, played pool, and held black-tie functions.

Though to that point I hadn't fully begun to notice the service workers on campus, I do remember a long night, at four in the morning, when Carol-Ann, the cleaning lady, came in early to get her work done so that she could get back home to take her kids to school. I remember seeing someone in the club lifting his legs momentarily from the table while Carol-Ann wiped beneath them.

The next morning I bought a tape recorder. Uncertain how to proceed, I let the interviews go in whichever direction they seemed to take us. The interviewing process made me a student all over again, and working on this book became a three-year extension of my official education. I felt humbled by the people who appear in this book in a way I rarely had been by my professors. I came away from interviews exhausted. It seemed to me there was nothing more complicated, fascinating, and problematic than trying to understand, and then describe, another person's life.

Some interviews were like conversations; some were more like lectures. Almost always, my assumptions and expectations were deeply challenged. To respect another person, I came to feel, was to acknowledge his or her complexity. I accepted that I might never understand all of what was said to me, and I came to appreciate how complicated the relationship was between workers and the beneficiaries of their labor.

At times, people's desire to talk seemed almost urgent. I was a passing stranger, but I could listen for hours, and often that was enough. More than once, I conducted an entire interview simply by pushing the RECORD button. Still, many managers and supervisors forbade workers to talk to me, despite workers' legal right to do so. As the Living Wage Campaign began to publicize these narratives, food-service and security companies contracted by Harvard, such as SSI (security) and Marriott (food service), forbade their workers to speak with me about work conditions. The policies were illegal, but their existence was difficult to prove because they were passed down to workers unofficially by word of mouth.

As a rule, the more protective the supervisors, the more I tried to get around them. With its lowest wages at around $7.50 per hour, the law school dining hall was the lowest-paying site on campus. It also had a reputation for disregarding workers' rights. Not surprisingly, its managers were also the most guarded and resentful of my curiosity. I had to wage a letter-writing campaign just to get permission to photograph on their property for a single day, and even then a supervisor decided to observe me quite deliberately. He sat hunched forward, taking slow drags on his cigarette, watching as I photographed one of the line servers.

"Do you ask them not to smile?" he asked finally.

I did not, I said, and controlling my voice added, "I let people look however they want to look." He threw his cigarette down and left.

The woman I was photographing, Mariam Nyota, was a refugee from the Congo who spoke very little English. I wondered how the supervisor could expect me to photograph her smiling. Mariam told me she was a single mother with three children, that her rent was

$1,100 a month, and that her monthly income was only $1,500. She was raising her three children on as little as $400 a month, that is, on an average daily budget of about thirteen dollars. She had let me take her photograph only under the condition that I would try to help her get into public housing. Later, when I called the Boston Public Housing Authority, I was told that if she wasn't already homeless, the wait list for her was at least two years. A year later, I went back to the law school to visit her; I had met someone at the Housing Authority who was going to help her. "She no longer works here," an employee told me, trying hard to keep the emotion from her voice. The rumor among the employees was that it was too much trouble for management to deal with Mariam's broken English.

From the perspective of management and those being served, service workers at large institutions are not really meant to be noticed; they are meant to get things done quickly and quietly. I wonder sometimes whether the limited interactions that do occur between server and served are so often superficial because they represent a relationship with which both "sides" are fundamentally uncomfortable. And yet, why do we seem even more uncomfortable when that structure is challenged? I asked that question of a library guard one day and got the following response: "Some people treat us like furniture. And if we do something to show that we're not, it really fucks 'em up. It's as if they feel irritated if I talk to them, as if they feel violated. Some people feel as though the person on this 'side' of the desk belongs in a certain role, and if you violate that, you're violating the status hierarchy. It really fucks 'em up. To the point where some people seem damaged by it."

This book is a collection of facts and feelings, served from one "side" to the other. The book is meant not to cause damage but to be an opening statement to a healthier dialog.

G.H.

The narratives in this book are edited transcripts of tape-recorded conversations. I read the transcripts many times, trimming them with each reading. I cut what seemed irrelevant or redundant; I left that which seemed eloquent, profound, and faithful to the ideas expressed in the original conversations.

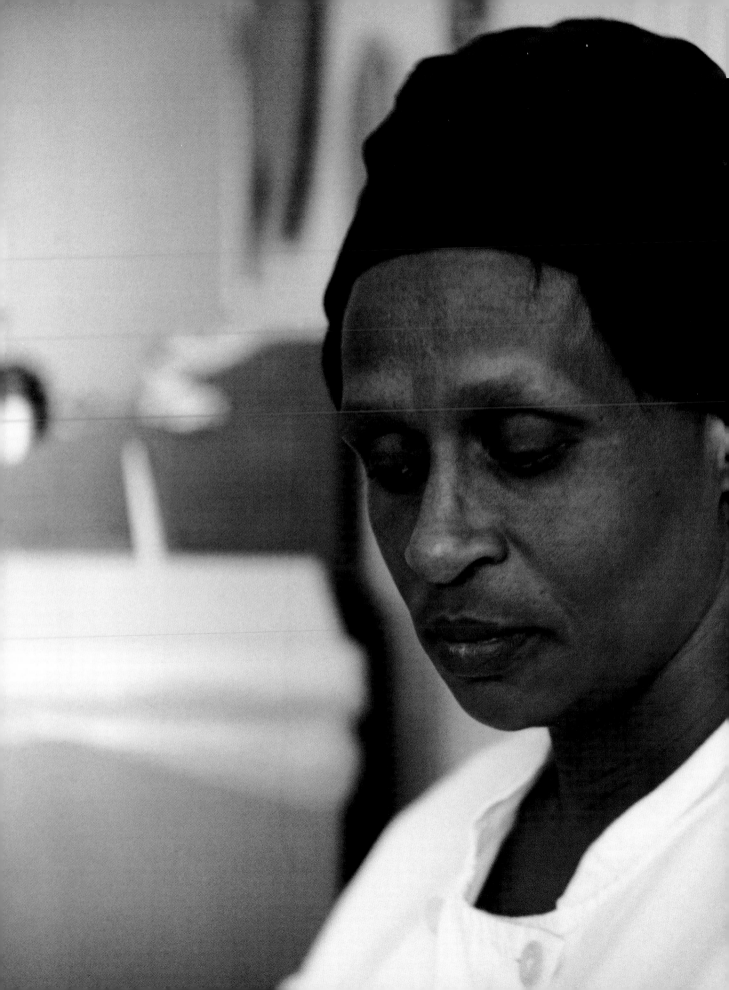

Mariam Nyota, Line Server, Harvard Law School

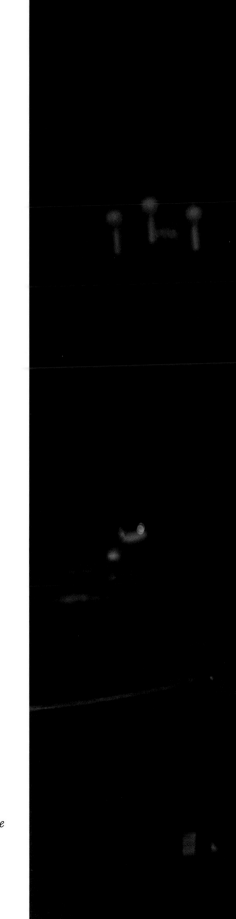

Tony Amaral, Chef, Dunster House

Wilson Saint Claire

Wilson Saint Claire

Custodian, Adams House

I was twenty when I finished college. Yes, I finished college. And the thing that is difficult for us when we come here is that no matter your class in Haiti, when you come here, you have to work as a cleaner just to survive. Some of us are high class until we come here, you see. In my country, they have a complex: if you go to college there, then you never pick up a mop when you come here. My old supervisor, he was from Haiti, and he was high class there, too. And so when I started, when I picked up a mop, he told me, "Don't think about it, Wilson, just do it."

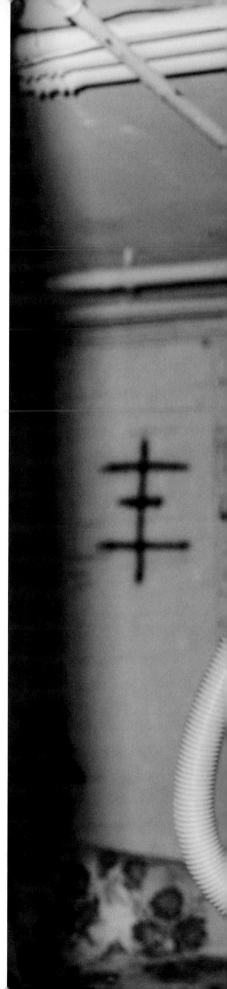

Carol-Ann Malatesta
Cleaning Lady, Phoenix Men's Club

The work itself sucks, all right? It's very tiring, and it's hard work, especially if one of the kids pukes. The kids drink, and they puke, and it dries on the walls and that's kind of gross. But you just clean it up, you hold your nose and you think to yourself, "I got three kids, I love my kids, I love my kids. I want the kids to be happy. The kids are going get to college! And they're going get pregnant by someone with a degree and a job, not like their mother!"

Financially I'm okay now. I was able to move out of the projects, but, you know, after paying taxes and day care and car insurance, that's when you start going to food pantries and soup kitchens at night and you start trash-picking for clothes and toys and furniture. I do it. It's fun—trash-picking. It's shopping. I mean, my kids don't really think they're poor. When we go to a soup kitchen, they think they're going to a restaurant. What the hell. It's free food. They throw it out if nobody eats it. We stick around until after dinner's served, too, so we can get a doggie bag to take home. Why not save it? Waste not, want not.

I find good food in the garbage here, too. Chinese food, you know—it doesn't go bad because of all the chemicals. If it's only been out overnight, I'll eat it. I don't care. I got some in the fridge now, if you're hungry. It's good. I mean no one puts their mouth on all the pieces. You can't get AIDS from saliva yet. I brought some home for the kids. "Hey kids!" I said. "I got Chinese food!" But, you know, at least I'm out of the projects. I had neighbors there who were selling drugs to try to make enough money to move out of there. They couldn't even feed their little kid, so I was feeding him, you know. Or I would take the kid to school, get him dressed, give him a lunch. I mean, at least I'm out of there.

It takes me about four or five hours to clean up after a party with all the cups and glasses the students leave around. Sometimes I come in at four in the morning and they're still partying. If I have a busy day with the kids and other jobs I have to come in that early so I can make it home by seven to take the kids to school. See, I was trained from a kid to cook and clean, to take care of kids. So now I'm just making money off it.

The thing I like about this job is I can come in here and talk with people from all over the world—from places I'll never go. Talking to the students keeps me sane; I go insane when I'm always working and taking care of the kids and I don't have any conversation. It's like I don't have a social life. This is my social life, talking to the kids. I don't have time to waste on dates. You know, I don't have time to come home from cleaning all day to sit there and wait for a guy to call me so I can go out on a date and act real feminine. I tried it a little in my early twenties. Even in college. But when you're going out at eight o'clock at night, and you got to be home by ten-thirty so you can be at work by four the next morning, are you going go out and talk for two hours and spend the night out and bring some guy home while the kids are sleeping? Come on.

I bet you're wondering why I'm not in a bad mood because of everything I have to do. Well, to tell you the truth, I think it started with my mother's husband, who was a jerk. He used to hit her, so she left him. And I was scared of all her other boyfriends, and I decided I was always going pull my own weight. I wasn't going to owe nobody nothing. Remember Shirley Temple? Every show she always said, "I'm very self-reliant, you know." I like Shirley Temple. She's cute. So I always tried to be like her.

Men have not helped much in my life. With men, it was always, "If you adopt me, I'll clean your house." I was a young girl, you know, and what happened is boom, boom, I started popping out the kids and then nobody was there for me. Well, I wasn't going let my kids sleep on the streets. I figure if I ever get homeless, I'll take over one of the rooms here at the Phoenix. This is a beautiful neighborhood! I have three kids—I don't want to be homeless. With kids, it's different, but I could do it myself if I was single and I had to.

I mean, there's good money in holding a cup in Harvard Square. You get your money that way, you put it in a safe deposit box. You go to the YMCA to take your showers, you go to work, you get your check, you put it in an ATM machine, and you sleep on the streets. Or you sleep in a homeless shelter. Eat in a soup kitchen. I don't mind someone taking from the system if it means they're getting ahead. Look at corporate welfare—it's corporate welfare that's taking all the money and there's no money left for the people. The government gives all this money to a company so they can come into a town, when in reality all the company does is cut jobs. It's amazing. Then those people start collecting unemployment, right? Keeping the poor people poor by throwing 'em some bones. We'll stay poor. Just throw us some bones! We'll eat 'em. We'll make soup!

I'm saving for a computer now, a fast computer for my house because the kids are getting into the Internet and if you want to get anywhere you need a good computer at home. I want my kids to go to college. And I don't think they'll get there if they hang out in public high school. I haven't sent one of my kids to public school. I went to Catholic schools. My brothers and sisters went to public and they started skipping school, trying drugs, goofing off, and what they were learning in the public high school, we got two years before in the Catholic school. The religion is nice, too, but that's not why. It's a better education. So

I've got my son in Catholic school. I don't have to worry about him. Plus, my son's not into sports. He's very quiet, not very sociable. He could not function in a tough public school. I think they'd eat him alive. So for me, it's about his safety and his education in that school. Plus it's cheap with the financial aid. And the girls are in a similar school, a prep school, but it's free.

My kids, they take Italian lessons on Saturday mornings. It's only a hundred dollars a year for thirty weeks. Two hours a week. Then I have them going to a church on Wednesday nights. It's Christian Cub Scouting. They do fifteen minutes of Bible study, then it's arts and crafts, and they do like the Boy Scouts. Except the Boy Scouts is run by the Catholics and it's like forty, fifty dollars a year, and this is run by the Christians, and it's only twenty-five cents a week.

When they get older, they're going be able to go to Italy with the Italian school for five hundred dollars for ten days. The Italian government picks it up. And then when they get older, I'm going to send them to a different church that sends their teenagers to different countries—and the church picks up the tab. Like, you pay five hundred dollars, the kids'll go to London for ten days and the church pays the rest. And I sent my son to Russia this summer with his school, because he's taking Russian for the next four years, and that was only twenty-three hundred dollars for ten days, which is a lot but it's also cheap, to go to Russia, you know? He went to three different places and he got to go to a Russian circus, and he got to eat the Russian food. So my kids don't really think they're poor. Like I said, when we go to a soup kitchen, they think they're going to a restaurant. There's a couple in Harvard Square we go to. You're helping somebody; somebody wants to feel good about donating the food, so eat it.

Being the cleaning lady, you know people. You hear things. You see things. You're the quiet dirt cleaner. I know a judge. I know lawyers. I know politicians. There's a student here who's the son of the guy who was the president of Egypt. I mean, that's a cool thing. I go around telling people I clean up after this kid. And they're like, "No way," and I'm like, "Yeah, I clean up after someone important!" I met him once and you know, he's just a regular kid. This club, the Phoenix, it's a big deal. It really is. It's just students now, but they know how to network and get things done, and they use the club and its connections and its alumni, you know, to make it big. And some of them have made it real big. This is the old-boy network. Harvard Phoenix alumni—I mean, these people are somebody. They got alumni making billions of dollars. I'm just hoping they remember me and give me some stock!

The Phoenix is all guys and I think it's better off that way. Men are basically easygoing. Women are complicated. They'll come in and change everything. They'll want to change the color, there'll just be more fights. Besides, that way I'm the only woman here—I'm special. They start bringing in young, pretty girls, I ain't got a shot, I got nobody to listen to me. The girls don't wanna listen to me too much. Plus, the guys wouldn't be able to talk as dirty, you know? They get all drunk, smoking their cigars, sitting in tuxes, telling these raunchy, filthy

The Phoenix Club

jokes about some douche-bag whore, right? You think they could stand up there and talk like that with women around? I mean, their jokes are funny. If I'd heard them, I'd use them elsewhere. But I hung around guys all my life. See, I'm single for two reasons. One is, men suck; but the other reason is, I don't know how to play the girl roles, the games that girls play, because I hang around with guys. Guys like to be the hunters to get the broads. If I'm out with a guy, I'll stop and be like, "All right, let's go," and it scares 'em, because they really don't know how to perform at the end—they only know how to get there! I'm just real cut-and-dry. It's different, I mean, you're not at that point yet. I'm thirty-nine years old. I can read people pretty well. And that's another reason guys don't like me: I can see right through them right away. I know the game, and I just ain't as much fun playing it.

I'm a battered woman, if you want to put that down. Overcome obstacles. I am woman, hear me roar. I will survive. "I Will Survive" was my favorite song for years. My first boyfriend—he beat me for three years. He used to choke me, mostly when he was drinking. Mostly he'd hit me where it wouldn't leave a mark. He only gave me two black eyes, so that's not so bad. I don't want to be dependent on a man like that, see? He started hitting me because I wanted to break up with him. He said, "You break up with me, I'll kill you." So I stayed with him for three more years—sixteen and a half to nineteen and a half. That was until I had the courage to break up with him, and I didn't get that until I went on this cruise with my girlfriend. See, she was getting beaten too. And when you hang with girls that are getting beaten, you just get used to getting beaten. Anyway, I figured he was going kill me eventually, and I wanted to go on a cruise with my girlfriend before I died. I even had insurance to pay for my burial.

It was a singles' cruise to Bermuda. Four days. Well, I met a guy there that actually talked to me. He looked at my face and he talked to me. And he kissed me real nice. It was nice, you know what I mean? He talked to me and he was really sweet. I mean, they're all after the same thing—it's just how they go about it that makes a difference. And he was so sweet about it. I remember thinking I was in heaven and that I could just die. We got to Bermuda. We were there eight hours. Then back on the boat and that was the trip. When I came back, I was so at peace with myself and very calm about him killing me that it scared him, I think. I was no longer afraid. I used to cower down, and they like when you go, "Oh, please no, please no." They love it when you beg. Because it makes 'em feel more superior. So I used to beg early, so he would think he's really hurting me even though he wasn't. But he could not handle the fact that I was not afraid to die. And then the relationship wasn't the same. He was almost uncomfortable around me. So we went on for another month, but we broke up pretty soon after that.

If you're wondering why I'm telling you all this, it's to explain that men have definitely not helped much in my life. My father, he drank. He has five children by three different women. He got my mother pregnant at age seventeen. After that, she was out of the picture, so he went and hooked up with another one. Here's a man who didn't pay child support, fooled around, lived his life the way he wanted to. And who's beside him at his deathbed? His three women and his four daughters.

My son's father, he's been on the Deadbeat Dads' list twice. He doesn't stay at jobs very long. And he never really visits his son. My daughter's father visits very little. We haven't seen him for years. And my last kid, the father comes around a lot but doesn't put any money out. He knows how to work under the table and duck his money. He's got no money in the bank and he's got no property in his name. Whenever he makes a deal and makes some money, he makes sure the deal is done in the name of one of his partners. The prick's got eighty grand, but on the books he makes it look like he's just got an increase in debt. I don't bother. I mean, if they don't feel that their child's worth enough to support then what can I do?

My grandmother used to clean, and she used to take us on walks through Harvard Square and we'd be looking at these buildings going, "Wow!" And I'd always say, "Boy, I'd love to get a Harvard degree," but my mother didn't raise me that I had any intelligence. She raised me to be a secretary and then get married. And it was always like only rich people go to Harvard. So it was a dream to go to Harvard. But working this job I get to be around intelligent people, and I like that—although I'm not always sure how intelligent they all really are. Like, I don't know if they're at Harvard because they're actually intelligent or because they have rich parents.

The students here are the politest people, though. I thought I was going be walking into a bunch of spoiled, rich brats who would treat me bad, you know? I wouldn't have cared, really, because it's just a job, but actually they're so polite. And I was really surprised at how smart rich people really are. I have a degree, too, so I'm not stupid. I have a degree from Bunker Hill Community College, and I'm finding out that I know a lot more sometimes, too, like I know more about life than some of the students. And that makes me feel better. That's life experience more than books. Life knowledge is more important; book knowledge gets you in the door. And quote me on that, all right?

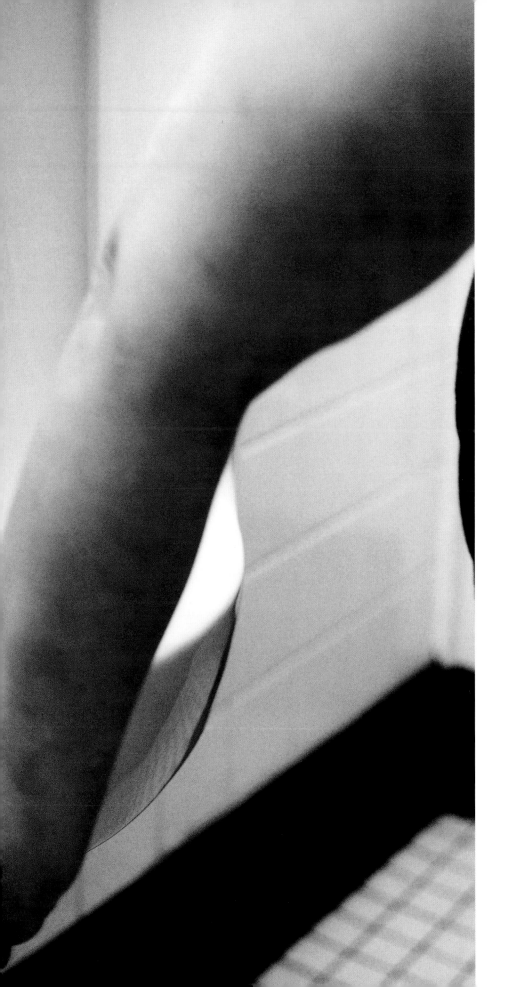

Bill Brooks

Custodian, Massachusetts Hall

Work is like a self-inflicted wound. It just is. See, I work for the president six A.M. to three P.M., I get three hours off, then I work six P.M. to eleven P.M. for UNICCO—that's another cleaning company. So I get home around eleven-thirty P.M, in bed around midnight, up again by 4 A.M. See, I am oppressing myself. And that's not normal, I know. It's just a rhythm—that working. That same old, tired same old. It's just a rhythm. And it's not normal. It's harmful to your psyche.

This here's just a job. It's just custodial services. But it's okay. It's all right. And it's not what you call "loving it." It's a just a job I'm paid to do. And your work is full. There's no what you call "idleness." It never slacks up. People are here at all times. I call it the Oval Office. You got people coming here from all over the world. And they have security, sometimes limousines or escorts from the Cambridge police, you know. This is like the White House here. It's a step up from most custodial work. Being in the president's office just demands more out of you. That clock behind me there, it's from 1712. I adjust that clock, and let me tell you, nine o'clock is not no nine-o-one. Everything is precision around here.

I clean, plus I take care of the staff. Anything that the staff needs. Take care of things, set up functions, tear them down. I just do anything the staff needs, see? Wash the dishes, teacups and saucers. Get more muffins and Danishes, clean the stairs, lock the doors, set up functions—anything the staff needs. Carry someone's books upstairs, bring someone's boxes downstairs, clean this fireplace, clean that fireplace, get more toilet paper—anything the staff needs. Everything revolves around staff. Anything they need, like, "Bill, I need some Xerox paper. Could you bring these books downstairs? Could you bring these boxes upstairs?" Set up for coffee, escort the movers around and the electricity folks around. I got a Director's Award, a plaque in oak wood, because they liked my work so much. I even got this letter of congratulations, signed by the president at the time, Mr. Bok.

See, they recruited me to work here, because they needed someone reliable, someone they could ask not to take the full vacation time. And it's tough trying to get someone to work on their vacation. See, I get five weeks vacation—because I been here at the university thirty years now—but I only take two weeks because they ask me to work the other three, you know. I don't even ask Harvard to pay me for the vacation time I don't take. Well anyway, they came and got me from the library where I was working, and you know how some people do—they sweetened me up with doughnuts and coffee and what have you at a long table like this. "You want more coffee?" I said, "Yes, all right!" And that's how they got me, if you know what I mean. And I been here ever since.

At Harvard, like they say, you don't get richer. Everyone knows that. The pay raises have been lower than the three percent rate of inflation, you know that? But you see, this building's got to be secure, so that's why they got these big metal bars over the doors and whatnot. It's a security measure. They got bugs on the key windows. They got alarms on the doors. They got police in here all the time now. This building, I don't know how old you are, but they took it over back in the Vietnam War. Then of course, you guys took it over during the whole living wage sit-in. That was serious, sure. And you all meant business.

I used to see President Rudenstine every day. Every day. Before that President Bok. Now it's President Summers. I used to take little envelopes from the presidents to all the deans so they could communicate throughout the university, from the Business School over to the Divinity School, this whole area over here. I used to take little envelopes advising them what and how and what have you. You know, a courier, in a way. What probably happened was they had some delicate stuff in those envelopes. But now they got what's called e-mail, so I don't do that anymore.

When I get off work at three, I go home and I bake my supper or something, because when I get home I got to have at least a meal. I live in Boston, see? So what I do is I go home to Boston, then I take the subway back here to Cambridge, Kendall Square, and I'll clean for UNICCO. And I come home at nine o'clock. So Saturday, you're tired. Gee whiz, yes. On Saturday, I wake up, I might read a little, but what happens is on Saturday you so tired that you sleep. You want to look at the TV, but you just fall asleep. I try to cook some stuff up on Saturday, eat it during the week. Sunday mornings, I get up early and I go to church, and it lasts until about three o'clock that evening. See, in order to not go through insanity, you got to have faith in something, so what I do is I go to church. See you get this monotonous continuity going on throughout your whole life. And that's why I go to church, to anchor on to something, to believe in something.

Happiness, I know—it's got to stem from something outside this working. I know I got to have something else to make me happy. I know you got to have your pleasure, but there's only twenty-four hours in the day. And there's not a lot of time left for that. See, one thing I used to do for pleasure was go to the movies, but I don't even do that anymore. A normal way of life is eight or ten hours of work, then you go to a ball game, a girlfriend's. It's not normal the way I work. It's too much. I started working like this in 1959. Workaholic— that's it, I tell you. Don't ask me, I'm no psychiatrist. But you know, you don't need no psychiatrist to figure it out. This is not normal. You got to sleep. What I do is like getting a boulder and pushing it up a mountain.

I just call it a depression state of mind. It's just a depression. I'm depressed now and I was oppressed before, that's the way I see it. See, I was born in Chattanooga, Tennessee, down in the valley, back in 1935, before King came, when segregation was a tradition, passed on since slavery times. It was just programmed to be depressing for blacks. That was the 1950s. Jim Crow. Back of the bus—back in those times you pay your fare, you go to the back of the bus. You couldn't get loans. You paid a different price for homes. Different schools. Education was bad. Different books for blacks, different books for whites. Believe me, it's depressing just to think about it. These are facts. This is not no novel. The only thing that broke it was Rosa Parks. And that's when King came in. I was fed up about the back of the bus, black toilets, white toilets, all that. I was fed up working at a restaurant, washing dishes, eating my meal in the dish room. You know, you can't go eat in the front of the restaurant.

Back in those days, it was pit-bull style. Everyone's uptight, feels like they been hated. You need that paycheck, that money to take care of the kids. It becomes a conflict and the conflict works its way into your family. Indirectly, anything you can think of, until there's no love there, you know? It seems what happens is, you start to wonder if someone could ever love you. I pulled my hair out I got so sick of it. I don't need this, I said. And I ran away from home. I ran straight away.

I got on a train, a boxcar. Came north. Your generation knows about planes, jets, and shuttle flights to the moon. But boxcars, see, that was as big as Delta Airlines in my time. My father was a fireman on the Southern Railway. Back in those times, you had to fire those boilers to move those locomotives. He went with the Southern Railway and we didn't live too far from the tracks, see, so he used to pack his lunch, take a walk, and in five minutes he'd be at work. Down South, most people, the black folks, they all lived around the tracks, more like the downtown. The rich folks lived on the other side of town.

But what happened, see, was I got my coat, got a skillet to cook on an open fire, a jar of water, some cinnamon rolls, and I just jumped into one of those boxcars at three in the morning. Everybody was asleep. I had got paid that night—fourteen dollars cash in my pocket. Fourteen dollars a week then—cash. I worked at some kind of white motel, working as a kind of busboy. Taking luggage up to the rooms and whatnot. And I jumped in one of them boxcars. I didn't know where it was going. I was thirteen years old—check my gray hairs, see, I'm sixty-five now and you do the math, check your math—I was thirteen years old. And I waited. I was there from three A.M. to three P.M. that day, waiting for the train to move. And the switchman, you know, he came around and he looked in there and he said, "Hey boy, what you doin' in there?"

"I'm goin'. I'm leavin' town," I said. "Well," he said, "have you been to Cincinnati?" "No," I said, "I haven't." "Okay then," he said. "We're leavin' in about five minutes." He could have put me in prison. He was probably an old redneck, too, back in those days. But five minutes later, the train started to move and I left for Cincinnati, Ohio. From Cincinnati, I went to Detroit. And I went by bus that time, no boxcar. I went by what they call a real luxury line. From Detroit I went to Concord, New Hampshire. Now that was a mistake. See, I wanted to go to Concord, Massachusetts, but I wound up in New Hampshire, in the White Mountains. I looked around and I thought, "This isn't what I thought it would be." I didn't see too many black faces, oh no. And people were lookin', too, so then I figured it out. Back in those days, blacks didn't go that far. Blacks usually stopped down in New York. I was the only black guy in that area. You know, it sometimes feels that way at Harvard, until you been here such a long time you find out that the staff are okay. I'm the only black guy there in Mass Hall, you know? Anyway, I was up there, and I was like, "Let's get out of here," so I came back down to Boston.

I got here and I lived off bread and water for seven days. I was sleeping in the train station. I was looking for a job. I was scared. First time out in the city. I found a room at the YMCA for two dollars a night. The woman there gave me twenty-five names from the classified ads, and I walked around town asking for a job. And I just put footprints to where I wanted to go. And it was the last person I went to that finally gave me a job. It was a restaurant, and I got there and he hired me as a dishwasher. But then I also made hamburgers and I worked as a soda jerk and I ran in the back to do the dishes. He needed me. Nobody else was gonna wash dishes and be a soda jerk at the same time. And he said, well here's someone who really needed a job, so he hired me.

After that, I figured I had to be conservative about taking care of myself, especially because I didn't know anybody in town. So I got myself a real full-time job. I looked in the paper and saw a sign for building storm windows. So I took that job, but I knew one of these days I was gonna get laid off, so the next day I went out and I got a weekend job as a busboy. I've always been that way. I worked two jobs ever since 1960.

That first year after I ran away, for the whole year I didn't even tell my parents where I was. I later found out my mom and pop were down home looking for my dead body, thinking I drowned—gone down in the quicksand. A whole year of them thinking I was dead. See, I was trying to hurt them, get back at them in a way, but I ended up hurting myself, and I always regretted it. I still feel guilty about that. Makes me feel like I been running for fifty years. It's kind of crazy in a way. Because they forgave me. They never did get mad. It's on me, really. See, if you do something bad to a person, if you got a conscience, it'll haunt you the rest of your life. Funny thing is, now I been feeling homesick, really. Homesickness—that's like an incurable sickness that only you know about.

That's why I work so hard. It's what you call escape. Workin' is just an escape. I know you heard about workaholics—that's what I am. That's why some people go to drugs. My escape is working. I don't have to work this job. I'm retired in July. I get a check. I get a fifteen-hundred-dollar check coming in every month Social Security. I work these stupid two jobs. You know it's not normal. They tell me, "Bill, you should retire." I've got money now. Gee whiz, I don't need more money. I got stocks. In 1969, I put five thousand dollars in. It's worth about a hundred forty-two thousand dollars now. It's not a money problem for me, no. I've been saving to buy a house, and I got that money now. I want to build a house back home in Chattanooga. Property. I want to be able to say, "Hey, I can retire now. I can do the norm, I can relax." Be down home. I got my brothers and sisters, everybody down there. I'm older now. Chattanooga, Tennessee, is where I should be right now.

I don't know how many more years I got, but I'll probably find me a wife and build me a house down there. I won't have to work no more. I came north to work and to save. And I worked hard and I done well. I made money. I been a busboy, a factory man, a cook, and a custodian. Valet in a white motel, valet in a black motel. I was a dishwasher—didn't have no automatic dishwasher machines—I was the dishwasher. Really, pots and pans. I worked and I saved some money, but that money, it ain't doing me no good. Not 'til I find a good lady to share it with. Usually people try to find a woman to take the pain out, you know, but that ain't what you call the answer. Some women will just make it twice as much. Here I am, I sacrificed all this life, just for it to end in some divorce. I could die of a heart attack tomorrow. But maybe I could find me a good little woman still. See, you get the lonesome feeling, you grit your teeth. Work doesn't give me satisfaction, no. But it's escape. By now it's a route that you don't have to think about. Numbness. Call it what you will. You go to sleep, and it's not there, but you wake up and it's there. And you got to refuse to give in to that hurt. Until I get back home I'm gonna always have that hollow void there. Working, tired, same old, same old, refusing to go and get drunk. But it's so easy to do that. Some people I know just turn to the drink. They go to the barroom. They go to the drugs—cocaine, crack. I could get me a bottle of JB scotch, let it roll off me like water off a duck. To soften the blow, you know. But you got to refuse.

It just shows that a person can become immune to anything. That's what you call willpower. Willpower—a lot of people don't got it. See, but I'm blessed with will power, determination, and stubbornness. It's a like a mule, you know. And it's not normal, okay? The way I work, it can be kind of hard to understand for a rational way of thinking. You know darn well that don't make sense. And I hope you can look behind the curtain, if you know what I mean. Because it's not normal. You've got to have sleep.

Bob Turner, Custodian, Maxwell-Dworkin Center for Computer Science

Marc Rose, Sous Chef, Harvard Law School

Ronald O'Neal, Chef, Harvard Law School

Lillianna Lenares
Custodian, Harvard Medical School

I tend to think when I'm at work, "God, I really don't want to spend six, eight, ten years cleaning." I think about my daughter, who has to wake up for school alone because both my husband and me leave at five in the morning for work. And every day I think about my parents, my brothers and sisters. And with the baby coming in April, I think a lot about her. I think about having to find someone to take care of her so that I can go back to work quickly, because I don't want to lose my three years' seniority. I have all the preoccupations one has as a mother. The thoughts come quickly, sometimes, but I do my job as best I can in as relaxed and orderly a manner as I can.

At first I had a strange feeling when I found out about the baby—happy and at the same time nervous. It was one of those things you want and at the same time don't, in part because it is important, and helpful, to raise a child among family, and it is only me and my husband in this country. Thanksgiving and Christmas are celebrated with friends, though I am grateful to God that we have such friends. For some reason, God decided to send this child when He did and, well, we must continue moving forward. I am not going to stop. I have my home to think about and I have Antoinetta, my older daughter, to think about. I do feel happy for Antoinetta, because she has been alone up to this point. In a sense, I am very happy. I welcome this child that God has sent me. I will have eight weeks off to receive pay at seventy-five percent. I will nurture the baby, and after that life will go on. I will go back to work. I will keep doing my job. I will keep doing it the best I can.

I clean a dining room, a kitchen, a meditation room, a small classroom, a small handicapped rest room and the area around it, two music rooms with pianos, one billiards room, a darkroom, another small rest room, a small living room called the Club Cougar, a chimney in there, and the Club Coffeehouse, where they gather at night to converse and study. Then I clean, mop, and pass the vacuum over a number of other areas. And once a week I clean the stairs. That is all. I have three and a half hours each day to do as much of that work as I can. I am usually busy, especially during the winter

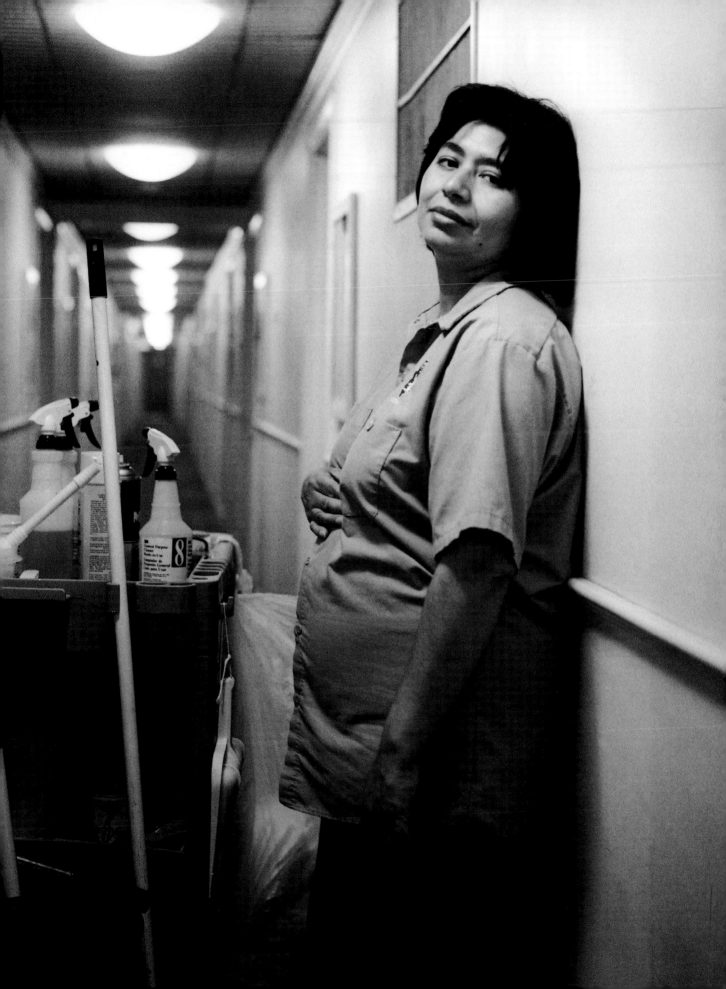

when it snows, then I have more work because they drag the snow and the salt in. That's hard, and when the students have parties they leave the trash full of beer bottles and sometimes I cannot pick the bags up. I just try to do my job as best as I can. I try to fulfill my duties. Sometimes they think that one is a machine. Sometimes my supervisor passes by and says, "You aren't going to do this?" and I explain that "Yes, I will do it," but there is a lot of work.

I would like a job where I did not have to expend so much energy, one where you do not have to clean the stains off the walls. I would like to improve my pronunciation. I would like to speak fluid English because once you speak English regularly you can find work in an office as an assistant or receptionist. I would like to study for a different career. There are people who get to age fifty and they are still sweeping. And if not sweeping, then it's passing the vacuum or mopping or dusting or cleaning out the trash or washing the trash deposits. But, well, work is work and in a sense I feel proud because I am earning an honest living—that is not embarrassing. The job I have does not make me feel less. It's an honest job. I would just like to develop myself further. And I would like to buy a house. I am an immigrant, but like everybody else I want to earn a better living.

I would like to not have to live with so much worry about every little thing, not to come home so tired, because money doesn't buy happiness, only comfort. Only comfort. One kills oneself working all the time and wastes all of life's moments instead of sharing them with family. I am thirty-eight now, and I think about my old age sometimes. It is far away but I can see it coming. I think about it at work. I would like to be with my family, to be with my husband and my little girls more. I envision my daughters as complete young women, working as professionals, married, with grandchildren, and a little house. Just a simple house, but a pretty one. A secure one. I see me and my husband, old and together there. Maybe a brother of mine will come and live there too. And God will be with us. And we will have our health. I have to think that way. I have to try to give my best. To share with others. And to struggle as an activist. No one has what they have today without pushing themselves, without struggling. Just because they are new over here, should they kill themselves as if they were mules? That is why it is necessary to struggle—but always with respect and cordiality. That is very important.

I hope my children will struggle and succeed. Antoinetta, she is thirteen. I want her to be good not only for cooking and cleaning. I want my daughter to be a professional. But I do tell her, "You have to be a professional." Those are, at the very least, the expectations I have.

*Claudia Flores, waiting in the home of Winthrop House
Masters while her parents clean the residence.*

Cindy Huff

Cindy Huff

Line Server, Adams Dining Hall

I was eighteen. I was all set to go to college. Maybe Harvard. I had one semester left in high school and they told me my grades were close. But that's when I had my stroke. And I couldn't go to college at all after that. If I had a chance to do it over again, I'd be a big shot. My sisters all went to college. Debbie went to Northeastern; she's a chemical engineer. Gail's a reporter on Channel Five. Jennifer got her degree in business—now she works in a corporation, and Callie, she's still in school. I'm the oldest. I wanted to be an architect. I do numbers easily. I got a knack. I'd have liked to be a math teacher, too. Probably about second or third grade.

My senior year, I was on birth control pills and smoking and I suppose that contributed to my having a stroke, but I was anorexic and bulimic as well, and I suppose that might have done the trick. I ate and I threw up, I ate and I threw up, and then each day I ate one meal I didn't throw up. When I was growing up I was in track and swimming and diving and gymnastics. Anything athletic I did. I was skinny, but I didn't see that.

My dad worked for the federal government, so we moved around a lot—Iowa, Nebraska, California, South Dakota, Mexico City, Boston. In a way it was nice, but we didn't have any place to call home, you know? You always felt like the new kid. Well, in Mexico, my sisters and I went to an American school—it was the kind of school for kids whose parents were kind of big in the federal government. I lived there for two years with my family. I think I was trying to get in good because it was the only school for us in Mexico, and if you didn't make it with the in crowd, it was kind of this feeling that you were nothing, you know? And I remember there were two girls that I hung around with that were skinny too. One was tall and slinky. She looked like she had the world on her shoulders. My sisters were skinny and taller than me too, so that didn't help. I don't know if I was just trying to get enough weight off so I would look like them—I don't know. Who knows? The mind can do funny things.

After the stroke I couldn't read. I couldn't write. My memory was shot. I had to go back and learn to walk. I relearned to talk. They said they didn't know if I was going to live or not. And if I did, they said I would never be able to learn to read or write, but I lived, and I retaught myself. I relearned to do everything. Just like a baby. My right arm is never going to get better, though. Just lays there. I was right-handed, too, but now I can write beautifully with my left hand, not cursively, but the other way. And my right leg is not as strong as my left leg and it doesn't point or anything like that. But I can work around it. Mentally I didn't get everything back, but I did get blessed somewhat—blessed because I got ninety percent of everything back. Took me about ten years or so to get there. And I'm still not fully recuperated. But I'm here now and this is the best I'm going to get.

The rehabilitation program placed us in jobs. I thought I was going to get a job at McDonald's—that's what a lot of the people got—but I got a job washing dishes at Harvard. And I'm still happy about that. If it wasn't for Harvard, I don't know where I'd be right now. McDonald's, I guess. That was 1982. When I first started, back a long time ago, I thought the money was good. Now I think the money is okay. But I guess at the time Harvard, the name, it just meant so much to me. But dishwashing is a hard job. Exhausting. So after about ten years, there was a woman who was doing the job I do now, and she left, and they wanted another person that was disabled to fill her place. But the old manager, he didn't want to let me have the job. And he had all these things written down like, "Can you do this? Can you do this? Can you do this?" And I said, "Yes, yes, yes!" And finally he had to give it to me. And that's how I moved outside—outside the dishroom. But it was a battle. Now they treat me like anyone else. They trample all over me! But people are amazed at what I can do. I can tie my shoe; I can play pool; I can ski, too.

I think I'm happy here. Keeps me busy. Oh boy. I get the bagels and the muffins ready, put out the peanut butter, the jelly and butter and cream cheese and so forth. The raisins, the dressings. Go in the back and get what I need. Turn on the steamers. Get breakfast ready. Fill anything that's gone. Make coffee. Put the bowls out. Get lunch ready—the ketchup, fruit, pickles. Notify the cooks if we're running low on anything. That's just what I do before seven A.M. Then we go eat. Then we start work again at seven thirty. I work six A.M. to three P.M. I wake up around four-thirty A.M. Go to bed by eight, if possible.

At work, I think of the students, I think of what they would want. I get them milk or soy milk or Lactaid if they want it. It makes me proud to get them what they need. I do a lot for the students, you know? So that they will be proud of where they eat lunch. Because I know if it was me going to Harvard, I would want everything to be okay, you know? Because you pay a lot to go to Harvard. And if you respect the students, they will respect you. Some people appreciate our work and some people don't. You just go with the punches. One day nobody's looking at you or asking you anything. Another day it's, "Hello, how are you?" And then it's, "Fine."

My favorite thing about the job is eating. My least favorite thing is putting the dishes up on the counter. The dishes are heavy. I'm forty-two now, and I thought I was going to work until I was sixty-two, but I'm probably going to work until I'm fifty-four or fifty-five because my arm can't really handle it. My hand is tired, you know, and sometimes it gets numb. I suppose because it's done the work of both arms for so long. So I put thirty dollars in my retirement account each paycheck, and hopefully when I'm fifty-four or fifty-five I'll have enough to retire. Or else I'll just switch to part-time. My dad bought me a condominium, and I just have to pay the fees. So I live there, in Acton, with my cat, Midnight. I watch a lot of TV. I hang out with my sisters when I can. I'm doing all right. I mean, I made it. And I'm still making it.

Judy Alford
Waitress, Harvard Faculty Club

I may not remember your name but I remember what you eat and I remember what you drink. That's the business, and this business is in my blood. I'm sixty years old and I waitressed in private clubs my whole life. My father managed a restaurant, my mom worked the same shift I do at the MIT faculty club, doing the same thing I do. My doctor says it strengthens—that it's a good body builder. I mean, you can't come in here and be some sort of a wimpy person. You won't make it. You have to have good shoes. And I wear support stockings, which are supposed to help, but the next morning you're always a little achy. But I figure that's what Tylenol's for. Plus I take vitamins. And of course a little caffeine doesn't hurt.

It's the running around, the always-on-the-go that gets you. If you go to the bar to get drinks for one table, you get them for two or three—save yourself extra steps. So each trip to the kitchen, do as much as you can on that trip, without hurting yourself, of course. And I've hurt myself over the years. We all have. I've pulled my back out before. Recently, in fact. So you just have to say to yourself sometimes it's not worth it, so instead of making it in one trip, you do it in two. With time, I guess, you just try to learn your physical strain. I work split shift—eleven A.M. to three P.M. and five P.M. to nine P.M. When the day's over, I come home and just flop—I sit down for an hour, I have a cup of tea, I relax. Then I'm okay.

The people have to eat and get served, no matter. So it's stressed—it's very stressed and you can't show it. You've got to get everybody what they want, and you've got to do it right. Your mind doesn't wander. You pay attention. It's a routine, an exact routine, and it's not really excitement. You try not to get too excited or nervous, because then you blank out, and you can't do that.

It makes me proud the way I do my work. The way I place orders on the computer, the way I satisfy my customers. Some people will say, "You take wonderful care of us, Judy. We appreciate it." That's rewarding for me. I enjoy the work, and I enjoy the people. I had a party yesterday of about five ladies. They called me over, and they said, "We just wanted to tell you, we think you're the best waitress at the Faculty Club, and if you ever need a recommendation . . ."

I please them. And it's satisfying to me. You have to be happy with yourself, and I try to be upbeat and happy and I think that transfers, because some people come in quiet and reserved and then after a while they kind of open up and seem more relaxed and more friendly. I kind of try to turn them around.

They just spent seven million refurbishing the place, so everyone who comes in here thinks it's beautiful. I mean, when the club's all set and done it looks really, really pretty. In a way, though, it never occurs to me. I've just been here so long. It's just a place of work—I go to work, do my routine, do what I do, and that's it—for twenty years. I know the club looks pretentious, but it's really not. It can be very warm. And the good thing is people can't just walk in off the street. So we don't have troublemakers coming in ordering us around—"Gimme this, gimme that." You have to belong here to eat here. And, if you've been staff at Harvard for fifteen years, you get a gold card, so you officially belong to the club and you can come in and eat, too. You still have to pay, but you can come in and eat. So then you're a member. I'm a member now. I can come here any time I want. And on your birthday, you get a free meal and you get to bring one guest. I actually went for my sixtieth birthday this year. But, you know, when you're in here working so much, you sometimes don't want to come back too often when you're not working.

I started at $4.43 an hour. That was twenty years ago. Now I'm making fourteen dollars an hour. They pay a little more because we don't get tips here. For whatever reason it's a nontipping club, and they don't want members tipping, so in the end it's not as good money as real waitressing. But I should be getting a raise in July. From the new contract we got a forty-cent raise, and that'll help a little. They say Harvard has twenty billion dollars in the endowment but, you know, the money never occurs to me. It doesn't mean anything to me. It never comes into play. It's not my money. It's a place to work. It's their money, and it's how they handle it, as long as we're being treated fairly and have job security. If you don't have that, you don't have nothing. And sometimes we have to have rallies to get what we want. We've never had problems—like no violence. But we stand up for our rights, and I think that's great. It was a good fight. I had one of those Tide cans with rocks in it, shaking it and making all this noise. It was fun, you know? If you don't stand up for yourself, who will?

I've been a waitress here twenty years and for thirteen years I've been shop steward of Local Twenty-six—the waitress and bartenders' union. In other words I'm the union rep at the Faculty Club, so whenever an employee has a problem, I file a grievance—and I tend to win. I want things to be fair. Thank God we have a union, really. Because when business increases, the managers, seriously, they're wrecks, and it just trickles down. I've been here long enough that I actually wind up training a lot of the managers that come in. And I can tell right away if they're gonna make it or not, too.

The best thing about the place is the customers. I've met a lot of real nice people. They've become like friends and they call me by name. John Kenneth Galbraith came in for lunch the other day—and God bless him, he's in his late nineties—and he'll say, "Hi Judy, how are you." I'll say, "Hi John, how are you," and so on. I've met a lot of famous people—Mel Gibson, Joan Kennedy, Joe Kennedy, Mr. Spock, Sean Connery, Sean Penn, Robert Redford. I like the one-on-one. If you don't like people, you shouldn't be doing this. I like contributing. It's satisfying to do something for someone besides yourself.

When I was younger I wanted to be a hairdresser, but then I decided I wanted to be a nurse because then I'd be taking care of people. So I took a job in high school working at a hospital. But you see, I got married very young, when I was seventeen. I was a baby, really. Maybe I could have gone to college, but at the time I wasn't thinking with my brain, I was feeling with my heart and I got married. If it happened now I might have waited a few years. But years ago, women didn't always get the education they get now. I had three children by the time I was twenty-three, so I was a full-time mom and I wound up taking part-time jobs to make ends meet—Fanny Farmer, McDonald's—which, forget it. I been working part-time since I was fourteen, and before that I baby-sat. Anyway, a few years passed and I moved up to the Union Club, then the old Republican Club in Boston—beautiful, old-fashioned clubs like here. And then I came to Harvard because I heard they had good benefits and my children were still little. My husband, he used to work one full-time job and one part-time job, but he was getting ill quite often because it was too many hours, so he cut down to one job, and that's when I started doing this full time. I had no idea I'd stay twenty years. There's only one other girl who's been here as long as me. Sometimes I think about how I wanted to be a nurse, take care of people. But the way I see it, I'm still taking care of people. I'm feeding them, so it's still taking care of them.

My husband passed away two years ago now, and between my income and his we did good. He drove one of those little buses for Mass General Hospital. But when he passed away, things changed. See, until then, I lived my whole life in Cambridge. Around the time he passed away, they raised the rent—from seven hundred dollars to two thousand dollars. Isn't that ridiculous? It's really kind of sad, I think. They used to have rent control because what normal person can afford two thousand dollars a month? I'd been here all my life. I went to high school two blocks from here, I raised my children here, and we all worked here. I didn't want to move. Not at all. But we had to. My son and I moved to Malden, and now it's about an hour and fifteen minutes each way to work and home. And I'm not really making any money now—after paying my expenses, I mean. And thank God I do have some savings because, if I need to, I can take from the savings and just match up with that. I'm lucky, too, because I have a two-family house, and with the rent from the tenant, you know, it pays the bills. But before, you know, when my husband was working, it was just fine—just fine. We were married forty-one and a half years. It's just me and my son now—and he's looking for work right now—but we're making it.

Rachel Herman

Chef, Signet Society of Arts and Letters

The Signet Society is . . . well, it's a so-called Society of Arts and Letters. It's a club that's meant for Harvard undergraduates who are "expected to make a significant contribution to the arts and letters." It was men-only until about twenty-five years ago. And when I first came here, I remember I felt very, very intimidated, because it was Harvard and because the Signet was, well, this very exclusive club. The Signet is a very nice place and it's just a very Harvard scene, you have to understand. I wondered whether I would be working with a bunch of people who were snotty. I was worried about the class thing, too, because I was born two blocks from the Signet, and I very much consider myself a local.

Over the last few years, I've become more acutely aware, in an ironical way, of what the Signet is and who I am here. The Signet is for students who are artists. Over the door, there's a sign in Greek that reads "Mousiken poiei kae ergazou." Various people have trans-lated it in various ways, but it basically means, "Create art and prac-tice it." That's the Signet's intention, and that's a great thing—they're going out into the world to make a significant mark in the world creatively. And I don't know if it's openly stated, but the assumption is that that's to help people in the world, to make the world a better place by creating something or entertaining people or perhaps pro-viding something sacred. But these people are practicing these art forms and yet, in a way, I am too. They do call it the culinary arts. And I'm practicing this art form right here in the kitchen and yet, the distance between us, the class difference, is so immense in so many ways. We're moving in different directions, even though we're doing the same sort of things. I don't know how to explain it. They're kind of on these layers or planes of reality that are really very different from mine. As if we're sort of moving past one another, like fluid dynamics, even though I'm a writer, too, and a poet, as well as being a chef.

There have been people who, over the years, have been notable exceptions, people who pointedly say something to the effect of, "Gee, you know, we should make you a member," or something like

that. I've asked my boss about it—about being a member—but I mean the reality is I'm not a Harvard student, I'm not a Harvard undergraduate, and it is intended for "Harvard undergraduates who are expected to make a significant contribution to the arts and letters." In a way it's funny that the students, who are sitting around networking, having fine conversation about fine art, they may not necessarily recognize that the very food they're eating is itself fine art. I'm constantly practicing my art, as they are, but I'm not a member. I think for the most part, the people who are members of the Signet, and I'm being presumptuous by saying this, but my impression is that they don't look at me as a creative force on par with themselves or their peers at all. You know, I don't think that even enters their minds for the most part.

In terms of how the students see me, I just don't think they give it much thought. Several of the students, the students who are officers, that is, have to deal with me when they have special dinners and so on, and they have to talk to me about what they want, and we arrange it and get the menu and they ask my advice. And I try to give them what they want. And I have very good relations with them and I've enjoyed being with them. But most of the other students, I don't even know if they know I exist. I mean, I think it's just—the food appears, and that's it. They're not here for me. I'm not part of that. I'm not important. And I'm not; the club is for them. That's the club. There's food here and that's all they need to know. They have their own agenda and their own reasons for being here and for being members and it doesn't have to do with me. It could be anybody behind that wall in the kitchen.

Again, though, there have been notable exceptions where, you know, somebody's struck up a relationship with me or really liked the way I cooked. Once, a woman said that my cooking was the highlight of her undergraduate career. And she said it in a piece of writing she didn't know I would read. I mean, that's one of the most wonderful things I've heard. I guess I tried to make the Signet one little place on campus where she could come and know that she was going to get something that was kind of comforting.

What I do is not considered great art. It's a very transitory art. It's here right now on the table. It's hot and it looks beautiful for a few minutes and then it's gone. I make my cakes beautiful. They smell like heaven—all chocolate and the finest organic butter from Vermont. I very seldom meet my own expectations. I try to do this thing with the food that really zips and makes it attractive and delicious and digestible and I try to get that "wow" from people. But yes, it is very transitory, and it's not considered an art form the way writing is—which it isn't. But that lack of acknowledgment is just part of the whole thing. You know, "The staff will clean that up." That kind of dismissiveness.

Now, interestingly enough, I've found that the people I've met, who come through the club from the British empire—England, South Africa, Australia, and so on—are not always like that and are in many ways the most comfortable with me and my position, as a staff person. They tend to say hi to me. They tend to find out what my name is and use it. They ask me how I am and they mean it. It may just be that more people from the British empire have been around servants and people who help around the house and whatnot. So it's not an uncomfortable situation for them. With the American students, I believe there's . . . there's more of an awkwardness there, maybe because there's a little insecurity, you know? I mean, after all, these are eighteen- and nineteen-year-old kids, right, and they may feel the need to do something to differentiate themselves from . . . from people who are not like them, to mark themselves as being members of organizations or cliques or whatever it is they think they should be.

Of course, I should also add that I truly believe some of the people at this club are amazing, amazing, amazing people. They play the piano or they act or sing or write these things. It's—they're incredible. And I love being able to witness any performance that they give. Sometimes I'll be cooking in the morning and somebody will be playing the piano. And that's, that's just really nice. There's a baby grand piano, and it's right on the other side of the wall from the kitchen, and so I can't always hear it very well through the wall, but I can feel it through the floors when they play it—through the wooden floor. Part of the reason I can't always hear it, see, is that I have a hearing loss. One day in 1992, I woke up and I had this tremendous ringing in my head. This ringing sound, for me, it's a high-pitched oscillation, an extremely high-pitched oscillation. I'm hearing it right now, and nobody else can hear it. But I hear it all the time, except when I'm asleep. I wouldn't mind losing all my hearing if I could get rid of it, but you can't. When I got the news, I didn't know quite what to do with it. It was devastating. But that's what the doctor told me—"You are becoming deaf." At this point, I can't hear speech in my left ear, and I'm losing it in the right ear, too. It's a long story, I suppose, but my point was that I can't always hear the piano. But I can feel it through the floor sometimes, and that's a wonderful way to work.

To a certain extent, if I'm in a bad mood in the kitchen, I think it influences what I'm doing with the food. And I don't want to be too New-Agey, but my energy has something to do with it. It's not just me, of course. It's not like I'm the all-important person in this chain. I'm just one in the chain, and this food comes from all parts of the globe. Farmers grow these strawberries, farmers grow this wheat, and somebody trucks it in their truck, and it's a complicated chain of all things for all this food to come together here on your table. I'm just this focal point for it to be put together on your table. I think I'm a transformative force, really. And then this fire, this transformation, has something to do with how people's days go. Some people say my lunch is the big meal of their day. They don't eat another big meal. And I prepare a five-course meal—soup, homemade bread, a salad or two, an appetizer, rice or some sort of starch, some sort of meat, usually a vegetarian entrée, and always some sort of fruit at the end of the meal along with dessert and coffee. And so when people go, "Ah! Wow!" you know, that means something. I try to make a happy little thing for the students.

The challenge of the job is that I don't know how many people are going to come until they show up. It could be twenty-three, or it could be forty. When that happens, it's important to have in mind what else I can either heat up or thaw out to put out there, maybe as an appetizer or maybe as another entrée. My boss, Mary—who, by the way, is the best boss I've ever had in my life—thinks I work miracles, but it's just thinking quick on your feet and having a plan.

That's not to say I wasn't very nervous when I interviewed with her. When I was hired, you see, I was hired with an agreement that the first two weeks were kind of a trial period. So I worked hard, and at the end of the first week, the people who were at lunch actually called me out into the dining room. So I walked out there and there were two full tables of people and they were all kind of crowded around one table and they were looking at me and then they gave me this standing ovation. I was totally—I was totally shocked, because I had never gotten any applause. I think that got me. That really touched me. I felt like this was a personal thing. See, I have to work in a place that I feel a sense that I'm affecting somebody's life in a good way. I have to feel like my work is intrinsically high quality, which, unfortunately, it is not always. I never really live up to my expectations on cooking the perfect meal and having everything ready at the right time and coordinated. It just never, almost never, comes out that way.

I feel this sense of irony because I'm one of those people who should have gone to Harvard or should have gone to some other school and gone on and done great things and so on, and, well, I'm sort of not. I'm sort of like this chef at this little club. And I make these creative little lunches and stuff. See, for me, there was a time when I was on the cusp of this kind of white-collar life; it was pretty clear that I was good with computers when I was younger, a natural, in a way, and I was all set for the executive, behind-the-desk computer-programming job. My parents were concerned for me. They wanted us kids to make money, but that's not what motivates me. It probably should because it really isn't fun to be poor, but I seem to have gone that way. By the end of high school, see, I was on course for college because I was supposedly bright and all that but I didn't really know what I wanted to do. So I went immediately into U. Mass Boston and I wasn't happy there. I left after six months and I went back to cooking. And I did that for maybe seven or eight years, until I realized how difficult it was to take care of myself and have my own apartment on the kind of education that I had, so I decided to go back to school. So I went to Bunker Hill Community College, and after that I went back to Tufts as a second cook, and I served about fourteen thousand meals a week.

Now, when I was working at Tufts, I was going through a transition—from male to female. It's something I wanted to add, but I wanted to save it for last. See, I was born male. This is strange stuff, I know, but it was especially strange to the people I was working with, because I went through the transition in this real blue-collar environment and it was kind of an unfortunate choice. I probably shouldn't have done that, but I did. I was instantly in a lot of trouble there as far as everybody was concerned. I was harassed about all kinds of different things, especially by one man who was a born-again Christian. It was brutal and I was actually frightened. So I left. I took a desk job for a while at FedEx, and after a number of years I left that job and that's when I came here, seven years ago, to the Signet.

I think there's a kind of smoke screen with gender issues, in the same way there is with class issues, where there's really little difference between inside and outside, but for some reason we feel we have to make a difference. With gender, men and women are supposed to be very, very different, and everyone accepts that. There are biological and hormonal differences and so on, but they're magnified and exaggerated to the point of almost caricature. Race is the same way—people don't like it when you're of an indeterminate race. And the same with class, where people try to fit you into these manageable categories that are safe and comfortable. When people first see you, they make snap judgments. Is this person a man or a woman? Is this person intelligent or not, working class or middle class? I'm in the in-between space. And the in-between space is not always a comfortable thing.

Kathleen Lenarcic, Line Server, Winthrop Dining Hall

Anonymous
Custodian

From the time I come from Haiti I always had two jobs. I work here from 7 A.M. to 4 P.M., then I drive a taxi cab until midnight. I come home around 1 A.M. And I wake myself at 5:30 A.M., because I have to be back here by 7 A.M. My family does not like it at all. I have four children, two boys and two girls—and they do not like it. My family sees me every weekend, but Monday through Friday I only speak to them on the telephone.

For a while, I took pills to stay awake, to be sure I did not fall asleep in the taxi. After that, I needed pills when I came home, to fall asleep. It is common, these pills, among the workers, but I rarely take them any more because it eventually makes matters worse. Working nights, the metabolism never quite adjusts. The nervous system is always a little off. But this is the thing: if you want to take care of your family, then you had better work two jobs. One job can't take care of nothing. And this is why I always have something on the side to do. If I go home and watch TV, my mind is always thinking of something else to do.

My struggle now is that because I have two jobs, I am having trouble controlling my daughter, who is a teenager. My wife starts work at three, which is when the children come home, and I am never home, so the children are liable to get into trouble without us there. My wife is trying to change her schedule, though it is not easy. I may quit the taxi because of that, though that will bring with it new problems. At this stage, for example, I do not even allow myself to cash my paychecks until the end of the month, because I am worried that if I cash it, I will spend it, and that there will not be enough left.

The summers are the hardest, because we do not work in the summer. The students go home, and so while we may know we have a job waiting for us in the fall, we lose our jobs for the summer months. Unemployment is not allowed, and sometimes you cannot always guarantee finding a job every summer. And so I feel the need to save for that, to back me up just in case I cannot find a job for the summer. They pay me twelve dollars an hour here, which many people say sounds very good, but again, I think the value of the wages suffers because we are sometimes unemployed for nearly four months out of every year.

I like to work for the students. I tend to like them very much. Though sometimes I notice they are afraid. Because for whatever reason I do not have to wear a uniform at work, and so some of the students will sometimes ask, "Can I help you?" or something. Because probably I look suspicious or something. And I say, "No, I work here." And they say, "Oh, I am sorry." I have noticed that when you put on the uniform, you become a different person. When I dress in a uniform, they never recognize me. But I have also noticed that it is the other way around, too. There are times when workers themselves only recognize you when you are in a uniform. Once in church I walked right by a guy I work with and he did not even recognize me, perhaps because I was in a suit.

I have been lucky, though. I have heard of people humiliated by students, but not with me. Because I know what I am—I am an employee. And I never mess with nothing between the two groups. Respect—the most important thing that you have is to show respect. All of the students in Harvard are very kind and intelligent. Give respect, and you get respect. And so I have no complaints. A friend of mine talked fresh to a student and he was fired. I never go far from my limit. My son is twenty now, and I think if he saw me get yelled at the way I do by my supervisor, I do not know. I would be upset. If he saw me bend to pick up the pennies, I would be upset. You see, the supervisors leave out pennies for me, on the ground, to see if I notice them and pick them up—to see if I have cleaned that floor carefully. I would be upset if he knew that. But even sometimes if my supervisor is being very hard, I try to keep my respect. I think there are many people who wish to say something, but there are also many people who work here who do not want to talk because they are scared to lose their jobs, or scared the supervisor is going to put more work on them.

It is not that I am not happy. I do not mean that. I am very happy here, and I mean that with my heart. The sad part is that I am happy right now, but if I get very ill I cannot work. In other words, as long as I can work I will be happy. As long as I can pay my bills I will be fine. Because the day you cannot pay, you are out in the street. You must work always. As long as you can work, you will be fine.

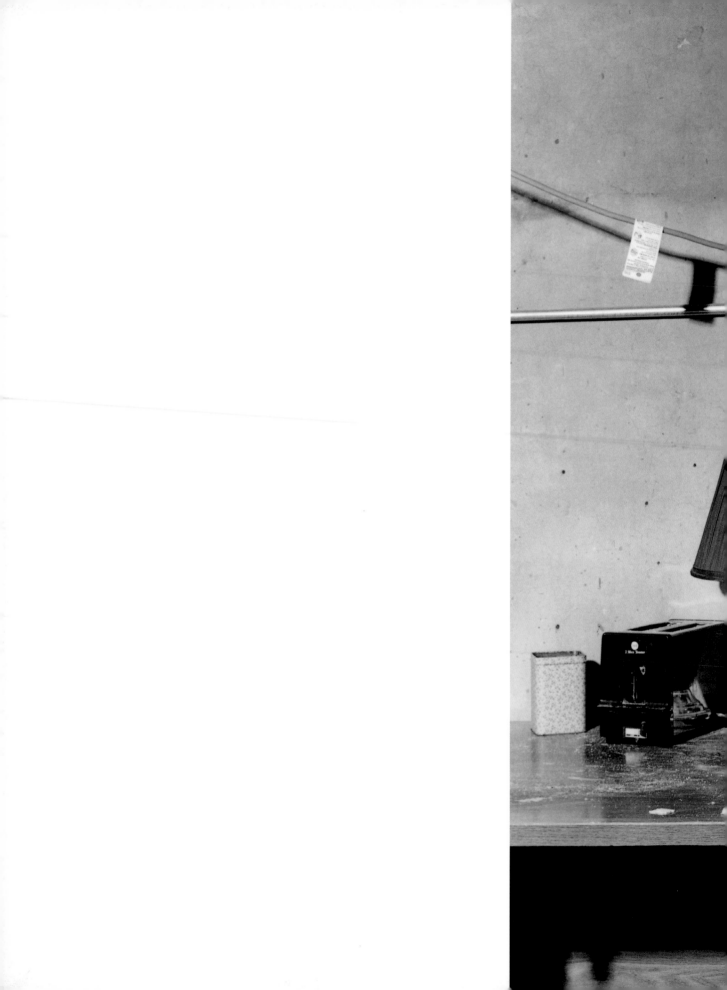

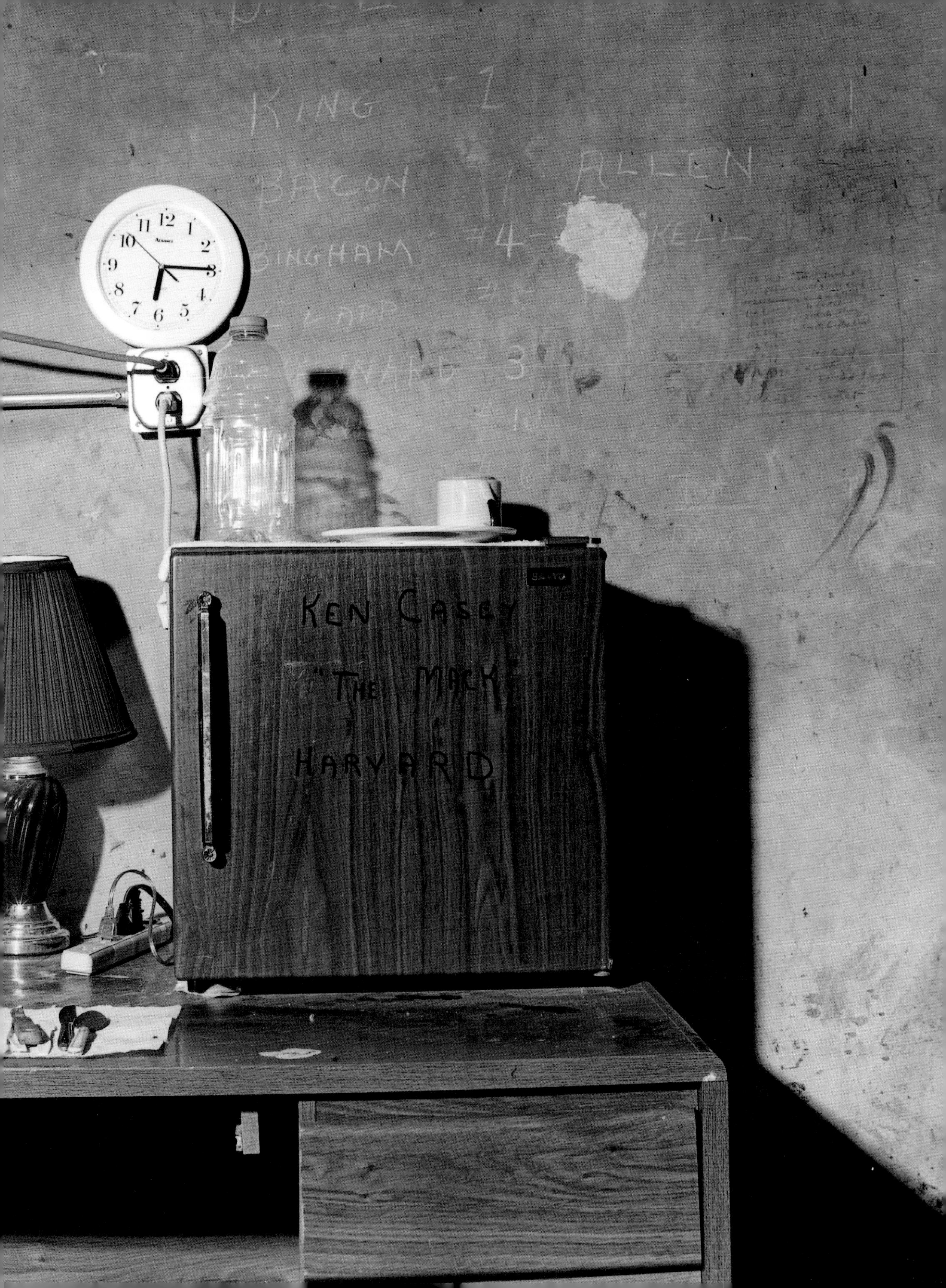
KING
BACON
ALLEN
BINGHAM
KEN CASEY
"THE MACK"
HARVARD

Anonymous
Library Guard

I got the job through a friend—a friend who knew there were people whose job it was to sit at the front of the library inspecting people's book bags as they left, and he knew the guy who hired such people. I had been working in a restaurant prior to that, preparing food, and I found that extremely hard. The labor market was terrible at the time. You could not get a job. Honestly, I was glad to be able to get in here.

The job is basically to sit at the door. But technically, there are a few sets of things guards do. The most important is to protect the lives and safety of the patrons and employees, but you spend almost no time doing this, because if you become aware of a situation, you simply call someone else. The second priority is to keep the collection on the shelves— checking people's IDs as they come in and inspecting their bags as they go out. Now, there's a third category of what this job entails, and it's the only one that's genuinely enjoyable, and that's giving people directions. Being people's guide. We have maps, we tell people where everything is, and it's—it's the only thing that people are very clear that they appreciate.

When you inspect their bags, for example, it's irritating to them in varying degrees. Every now and then, you come across a person who realizes that the materials they need would not be there if bags were not inspected, and I appreciate that, but those people are rare. Most people are tolerant—they're tolerant of having their bags inspected. A lot of times they're annoyed. And that's the burden of the job, that emotional response from people. You get a varied response. Sometime some guy'll strut up wearing a suit and an attaché case and with one sweeping motion put it on the desk and pop it open and there it is, and he's there talking to another guy and he's totally unconcerned. Now, sometimes with women, the search is more intrusive because you inspect women's pocketbooks, and every now and then there'll be a woman who clearly feels violated by it. That's uncomfortable. The choice is either you don't inspect thoroughly, or you do and you just try to be fast. I find that with most people, the intrusion is less intrusive if you're in and out fast.

There are, of course, uncompromisingly congenial people too, who cannot pass by another human being without saying hello, and that's nice. But some people treat us like furniture. And if we do something to show that we're not, it really fucks 'em up. It's as if they feel irritated if I talk to them, as if they feel violated. Some people feel as though the person on this "side" of the desk belongs in a certain role, and if you violate that, you're violating the status hierarchy. It really fucks 'em up. To the point where some people seem damaged by it. So what I do to survive is I don't challenge the people who treat us like furniture. I have the noncommittal response that they expect from me.

I'm currently a "casual," meaning I work under seventeen hours a week with no benefits, which I think is wrong. What I do about health care is that since my income is low enough, I qualify for the City of Cambridge free health care. A few years ago, before the city got rid of rent control, the money I made here would pay my rent and food, and then if I got some freelance work, I could buy some new clothes and go to a movie. But when rent control ended, I was in trouble. So I went to the city Housing Authority, and that's how I wound up living in public housing. My rent is subsidized by the Fed, and the deal with my room is that you pay thirty percent of your income.

I took the job, you see, at a difficult point in my life, and as a kind of survival job, and it's been a point of stability in a sense. A lot of people do take these jobs for that reason. And different people have different responses to it. Personally, keeping the collection on the shelves is something I can relate to, especially as the world moves toward electronic technology books become more and more valuable. Once they're gone, destroyed or stolen, they might never be seen again. People deserve not to have to look at a CRT monitor all day. They deserve to see a piece of paper in a nice binding. But some people just decide that it's a dumb job, it's a stupid job, and they're not going to take it seriously. I can't work that way. In order for me to stay sane, I have to do it well. I agreed to do it. I told them I would do it, so I have to do it well. I have to be thorough, I have to keep the collection on the shelf. If I'm going to decide that the job is just too dumb, then I'll have to quit.

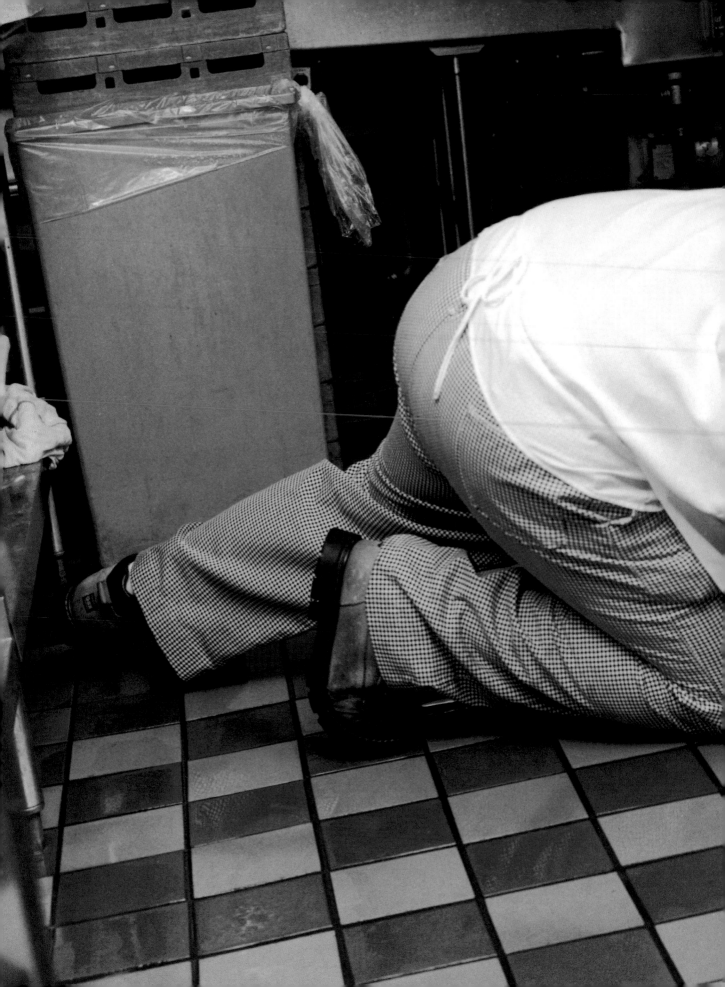

Anonymous

Custodian

I am invisible, you see. Let me explain. Where I work, there's this very tall, very pretty blond girl. I see her all the time, but she never sees me. She sees through me, if you know what I mean. The first time she saw me, I was cleaning the women's bathroom when she walked in. She asks me to leave the bathroom, because she has to use it. So I walk out and I wait a long time. When I go back, I find out she had not even flushed. So I'm there in the bathroom, and I'm asking myself, "What are you doing here?" And I say to myself, "Okay, what I'm doing here is a job, and I've got to do it, I've got to do it." So I flushed it and I cleaned it. And I'll clean it again if I have to.

Now, after that happened, a few days later, me and this girl passed each other in the hall. And she didn't see me. A few days later, the same thing. Now, you have to understand that there's something I do when someone ignores me like that. You see, one of the offices I clean has the student files in it. And don't think I'm crazy, but I have this funny habit where, if someone really does something that's bothering me, late at night when I'm working and when everyone's gone from the office, I'll go to their files, see? And it kind of makes me feel better. So a few days after this bathroom thing, I went to her files and in a few minutes I knew everything about her. Test scores, letters of recommendation, that stuff. Her parents were very rich—I remember that. So I figured someone like me is probably nothing to her. Maybe to her, I'm the same thing she left for me in the bathroom, you know?

I tend to think about those things over and over again. Ten million questions. "Why did that person do that?" I don't get angry about it, really. It's just, there's lot of time to think over the course of a day. So you think, and then sometimes you do these things. Anyway, I had been thinking about this whole thing quite a lot, until one day a few weeks later when I'm at my other job—I wait tables, that's my second job—and I see her, sitting at a table. She wasn't with anyone. And I immediately decided I wasn't going to take her order. So she waited. Until I thought the best of it, and I go over to her table. She starts to order but I can't seem to write it down. I look at her and I just start telling her about herself. I give her all the information: "You're from this town, your mom's name is this, your dad's name is this, your last college is this." Anyway, I think I scared her, because she starts asking, "How do you know me? How exactly do you know me?"

And I just say, "I do not know how I know you." And then she got up and left the place. And the amazing thing is, I thought after that she'd see me, right, and get me in trouble. I thought I'd lose my job, actually. But she still never noticed me, not even once, right up 'til the year she graduated.

Anonymous
Facilities Maintenance Technician

You have to understand that there's basically a code of conduct at Harvard, and one of the codes is about participating in things that question the university. Years ago, for example, during the protests about Harvard's investment in South Africa, I just wanted to go down there to see what was going on. I was curious. But they didn't want us going anywhere near there. There were students camped out in the yard for three or four weeks. And when I used to pick up my keys at the administrative offices, they would say, "Don't get into contact with them, don't have a discussion with them. Just ignore them, okay? Just ignore them. And don't talk to anyone from the student paper, don't talk to anybody. That's it."

You know, it's not always about overtime when you get called in to work at three o'clock in the morning, and get out of a warm bed because someone here had no heat. I do that not because of money. I do that because I work here and I respect that I have a responsibility and a commitment to Harvard. I consider myself very loyal to Harvard, but I do feel I have to say something about how there's this sense that if you speak your mind about Harvard, you'll be taken care of. They may not fire you, but there are plenty of other subtle treatments.

Like with the Living Wage Campaign, we were told again, "Don't be down there. If you're down there, you're going to be noticed, and someone's gonna check your time cards." We normally get paid for our lunchtime, but they basically said if you're seen at the rally, your lunchtime pay will get docked. So I'm just saying Harvard takes its image very, very seriously. They're not evil; they're just a well-oiled machine.

Mike Cunningham, Server, Private Catering Service

Wayne Murphy, Dishwasher, Harvard Law School

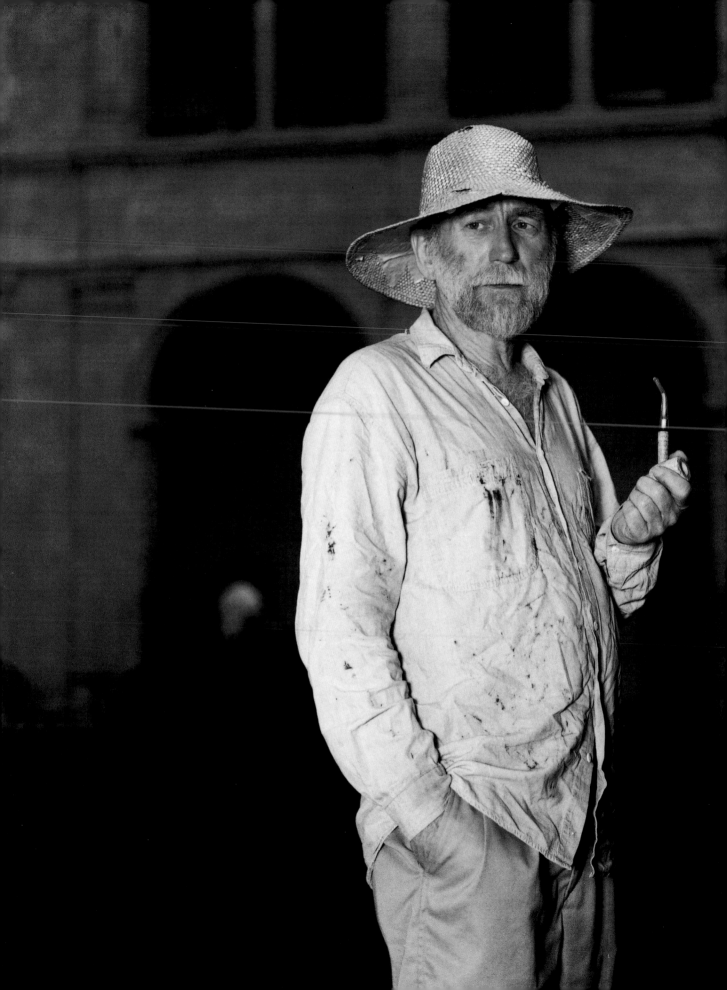

David Noard

Security Guard, Fogg Art Museum

There's a reason I've got hope and I'll tell you why. I've got something I love—I call it my Vincent Project. It's a two-part project, and I've been working on it five years. The first part is a book I'm writing about Vincent—Vincent Van Gogh. The second part is a one-man play about Vincent. I've written it and I perform in it. I perform at parties, mostly, and at assisted-living homes, though I'm working on going to off-Broadway, Tokyo, London. I'm taking a leave from work soon to do a series of performances down in Florida.

I'm in debt, see? And it's all debt that amounts to money spent on the Vincent project. But the project, see, the project is how I'm preparing for my future. If I sell my book, in other words, I just might get to work a few years short of forever. I'm sixty-one now and I'm really busted. I literally have no money.

At the moment I make $9.40 and I guard millions and millions of dollars worth of art. My daughter works as a clerk in a clothing store and makes more than I do. It's very, very difficult. $9.40 is not enough money to live on. Working overtime is how I survive. Five years without a raise. We got a $200 bonus once. I did the math and it amounted to three cents an hour. At this point, and at this rate, I'll work forever. I'll never retire. And if for some reason I really had to retire, I literally would have to move to Indonesia. I'm serious. All I would have is Social Security—about ten or twelve thousand dollars a year.

I grew up in a small town in central Illinois. Mostly I was bored and frustrated. I had no real sense of who I was. I drank too much. I went into the Army. I dropped out of several colleges. It wasn't until I went into the real estate business with my brother that I finally felt settled. I was buying properties; my brother was a woodworker and we'd refurbish them. I was happily married with one child and another on the way when it all sort of came to an end. What happened was I fell into a depression, fell into a state where I couldn't manage the business, and one day, it all just broke, fell apart—I lost a half a million bucks in one day.

It was a crucial event in my life, and it actually led to a very positive change. It was after that I went to talk to a psychiatrist who gave me a battery of tests. The tests told me I had ADD—Attention Deficit Disorder. Now, short of having two kids, this was the best news I ever had. I'm sure now that over the years, ADD was seriously affecting my sense of self. I was furious at certain times in my life, and at intervals I was depressed. And then, my doctor explained that much of that may have been due to this disorder. My whole life I had never been able to focus. I take four pills a day now, and I'll tell you, I can focus.

But most importantly, it's affected me in that sense that I've been able to create. See, years ago, I studied photography at the San Francisco Art Institute. And I loved it. When I moved here, I took some art theory courses and I really found that I loved it as well. But I literally had to read one word at a time, like *See-Spot-run*. My parents used to chastise me: "Why don't you just try, David?" But it literally was impossible for me to do the work. And I got fed up of being treated that way. Now I see that I can make a go of it. It was after the diagnoses of ADD that just bubbling out of the ground came this two-part Vincent project—a play and a book—totally, all so completely clear to me, so I went to Amsterdam and the south of France. I spent just sixteen days in Europe. And this was not a rational process at the time. Vincent can be a hook to straighten out some mental health issues. He's a natural, and I feel strongly about self-expression. I see now that if you're afraid of something, it doesn't mean don't do it, it just means you're afraid of doing something, and go ahead and do it.

What's come out of this all has been this biography of Van Gogh as well as the script for the play. I live in New Hampshire now, and that's where I do my work. I've adjusted my schedule so that I can cram a full work-week into three days here at the museum—Monday, Tuesday and Wednesday. I stay at a friend's house Monday and Tuesday nights, and Wednesday after work I'm back to New Hampshire, where I spend the rest of my week working on my manuscript. The book's not complete, but it's getting closer, and it's given me something to feel quite good about. Without me asking, the curator here even edited 125 pages. A hell of a compliment, one hell of a compliment.

I'm preparing for the project's completion carefully. When I can, I use my time at the museum to work on my lines. I carry the lines in my breast pocket and I memorize them here, when I'm allowed, but most of the time reading is not allowed, and there are cameras to check on you in every gallery.

I'm not saying the museum doesn't have value to it. For example, the Ben Shahn exhibit that's hanging now, they reconfigured the entire interior structure of the room for that exhibit. The central painting in that exhibit, there's a real chaos and energy to it, and they structured the entire room to match the feeling of that painting. They do something along those lines for every show. The department that's responsible for it all is really ingenious.

You know, I am grateful to have a job, but to be truthful, this job ultimately has very little value to it. I still get exhausted or fairly depressed, and I'm still furious that I'm underemployed. As I said, I'm broke and in debt and I may never retire. But what helps is that I'm actively engaged in my future now. Of course we need better wages, and of course Harvard can afford it.... It's just—it's just such a different fate so many of us have. The students, whether they are conscious of it or not, are really very privileged. And they just had the good luck to be born of these people who have some brains. It was all an accident. It's like one of the lines in my play where Vincent says, "I have no responsibility for why I'm here. I'm just here." He understood that he didn't choose to exist. He chose to live or die after he existed, and there were times he wished he could will himself out of existence, and he eventually did. But we are accidents. Vincent felt that keenly, and so do I.

Angel Hernandez, Waiter, Faculty Club

Sochea Uel, Dishwasher, Winthrop House

Shakespeare Christmas

Custodian, Paine Music Hall

When I look at the history of the entire world, it is one in which the older folks, the parents, put their knees on the ground to scrub the floors and do whatever they have to do to help their children. When I came to the U.S., that is what I had to do for my children. Now I am fifty-four, and I can say that even if I die at fifty-five, I have at least given them that chance. You see, one of my father's loves was history. And I know for sure he studied Shakespeare and that he fell in love with the name. I am sure my father was expecting much more from his children. I believe I disappointed him, yes, but in the next four years, you see, we will be graduating the first lawyer and the first two doctors in the family, and through my extended family, we have about nine high school and college graduations. And so I am beginning to think that wherever he is, he may begin to feel a little more proud. While most of his imme-diate children did not do too well, the second tier of the family is picking up quite well.

As soon as I came to the U.S., I was fighting with myself as to whether I should go to school or whether I should bite the bullet and go to work. But it was quite clear that I had to go to work. I had to raise the money to bring my wife and the three children here to the U.S., and to send the children to school. And so I decided to give them the chance. It would have been selfish for me to go to school. All of us would have been sitting in the same classroom wondering where we were going to eat that night. And so I came down here to do the dirty work, to pick up the trash. But God forbid, I told myself, my children will not do this. I swore to my three children, somebody will die—between me and them, if one of them were to come and do what I am doing. It is a job, and somebody has to do it, but I ask God every day, Why me? I live a miserable life down here. I'm not going to kill myself over it—things are already like this. I did the best I could possibly do, and they have all turned out quite well, and in that way it is not total shame.

Sometimes, doing this kind of work, I think to myself, "If I had gone to school, I would not be here." And you feel angry. You feel bitter, somehow, every day. It is my job, you understand, to wake up at three o'clock in the morning, every morning. The alarm blows, and I get ready between three and four. At four-fifteen, I leave the house. I get here, and I clean this building—Paine Music Hall. I do whatever I have to do, and at one-thirty, I head back home. By two-fifteen, I reach home. I lie down for an hour, an hour and a half, I stretch my legs, and at four P.M. I go again. I go out to the second job, just as my wife is coming in. My second job is at Children's Hospital, doing to same dirty work. I work from five to nine P.M. I leave there at nine, get back home, take a shower, hit my bed by ten, ten-thirty. And I am ready to wake up again at three the next morning. That is the routine. On the weekends, I tell you, it is so nice that I never leave the house even once. It is not only difficult to work in a school and to be surrounded by students, it is a shame. It is a shame to be doing this in a place like Harvard where there are so many people with high educational status. Sometimes you have to swallow the shame. Sometimes you have to swallow the shame and accept that it is a blunder in your life and one that you have to learn to live with. I am not blaming the students, under no circumstances. But in some sense, you are looking at the students, saying to yourself, "I could have been there."

I see nothing proud in this. I know in some buildings, people give you a look, as if you are someone of less value. In my building, they give you respect. But there is nothing else, absolutely nothing else, to make you feel an inch, or if you want to call it proud, or with any sense of dignity. In a country like this, no one should be working a forty-hour week and cannot pay their rent when the month ends. If the system asks you to work a forty-hour week, that week should compensate you for your basic needs.

I grew up in the Commonwealth of Dominica. I was a farmer, and so was my father. I must tell you, my dad was not universally educated, but he was not a fool. He grew up poor like everybody else, but he always said to his children, "Once you are educated, you are rich." If he had a book, he would cut it in two, to give each of the children a piece to go to school. If he had a pencil, he would cut the pencil in two. There were school years, yes, but it was just a name—"school." If you happened to go there, you got one reading book, which three or four students had to share. Those of us who were not so bright fell in the cracks, and that is where almost all of my mother's children fell in. I consider myself to be an illiterate. People tell me I am not supposed to see myself like that. But I still feel there is so much that I could have achieved. My brother is an accountant. And of the fourteen children, he was the only one to make it through high school. Call it what you want, but the rest of us are illiterate.

Back home, the way school worked was that the whole town would send nine or ten children to take the high school exam. Of those who took the exam, maybe two would pass. The moment the child got the news that he or she had passed, their parents would rush to town, which was twenty-one miles away. They walked on a track, a path, because there was no road, no telephone, no radio, no running water—no nothing. The path passed under the bushes, over precipices, the river, the valley, and the mountains to get to the town. They walked as quickly as they could, to try to get a spot for their child in the school. The school had a certain limit, you see, and always, more people passed the exam than could fit into the school. So sometimes, if the parents did not reach the school early enough, their child would not always get a spot. But if the parents did find a spot for their child, they next had to find someone living in town, and would pay them to let their child stay with them. Soon the child moved to the city, and lived there for school. After that, if there was moonlight, the parents would walk back to the village that night.

I did not take the exam. I was not that bright. And I believe there were only two children my age who excelled, and looking back, you can see that those were the extremely bright ones. In 1954, the very first person went to high school from my village. I know because I am married to his sister. As for me, seeing as though I did not make it into high school, I found a job doing masonry. I was sixteen years old, and I had been learning masonry for approximately one month when my father got in a car crash and died. From the day he died, I stopped the masonry. I had to take over the farm because I was the big one in the house. I took over full responsibility as a father, a husband, a big brother. My father—he grew the crops to feed the family. He raised the cows, the pigs, the goats, the chickens, the black cat. On Saturdays, he went to the ocean and would catch enough fish to last until the next Saturday and beyond. And so now I had to take over, to care for the little ones after me.

Now, by the standards of Dominica, I was considered blessed; my father had left me a piece of property for farming, a piece of land that was cultivated already. All I had to do was maintain it, and that was considered a good living. That was what everybody else had to do, and nobody in the community had anything much better than the others. For example, you can count the number of people on your fingers who held a steady government job. I farmed for many years, until the family was situated and I had the opportunity to go to the U.S. And if you get the opportunity to go, you go.

The only problems I ever had with my children was when my youngest daughter was seventeen, she thought she did not want to go to college. She said I was forcing her to go to college. All along, she was the brightest of the three, and so we had a serious, serious talk, and I actually cried to her—physically cried. I could not understand what was in the outside world for her. "If you do not have a degree today," I told her, "you will be standing behind a cash machine in a store where the boss pays you whatever he wants to pay you. Take a look at your mother and your father." When a child falls in the cracks like that, you may see the father walking on the street with his head up, but when he lies down at night, when he finds himself alone somewhere, he is crying.

My son graduated from ITT Tech. He works for a company fixing electronics. My first daughter, she is a project manager for Fidelity Investments, and my second daughter, she is working at a company that makes medical equipment. I have every reason to believe that they are doing well, and for that, I thank God. They are my sun, moon, and rain. I consider them my riches. I invested in them. And like I told them, although I am still mobile, sooner or later I will become disabled and I will expect them to buy me my prescriptions and to at least give me something to eat.

In the case of people like me, I do not think there is much of a lifestyle to look forward to, not other than your daily survival, and that is why I am still working at the hospital—it is an investment I can fall back on when I get too old to work. I would like to retire back home, in Dominica, and grow fruit there if I still have the strength and enough money. Until a few months ago, you see, I had not saved one penny, not a single penny. The children were in school. I do not know what it is to go to restaurants and eat. After being here seven years, we did go out for the first time. And now we treat each other on special occasions, on graduations and on birthdays. My wife cooks every day, and we are very careful to not waste money.

For those of us having to do this kind of work, it is just to survive, and I don't think the Harvard administration understands it. I know because I was part of the wage-negotiating team for the custodians. For this kind of work, they say, "This is what the market can pay you. And what we pay is what we pay." But there are many small things they do not understand. For example, I cannot pay four hundred dollars a year to park my car, so I sacrifice more sleep to come down in the morning to find a spot. They do not understand about sleeping four hours a night. But these are facts. When you sit down around the lunch table with the rest of the workers, these are the stories that you hear. These people who come and clean your office and where you live—they come with a smile on their faces, because that's all they've got. On Thursday when they get that paycheck, they cannot buy a cup of coffee. If they cash that check and buy a cup of coffee, then something else will be short—the light bill or the rent. I mean this in the literal sense that they cannot buy a cup of coffee.

Now it is twelve-hour days for me, because the sixteen-hour days took its toll. Back then, I could not sit down five minutes without falling asleep. I used to work at the Hyatt from eleven P.M. to seven A.M. And I was supposed to work the cleaning job from seven A.M. to three P.M. Then I would go home, eat, take a shower, and go to bed so that very soon I could wake up before ten o'clock that night to go back to work. I was so busy I rarely saw my wife. My children were very upset about this, the little one especially. She began to get very upset if I would go out at all on the weekends, even if it was just to see my brothers and sisters. And my wife, she is a saint. I do not know how she tolerated me.

Let me say again, the intelligent person will sometimes accelerate himself to a higher position. The mediocre one will always fight to survive. And those who are not bright will be down there scraping the surface to survive. Me, I am the mediocre one, the one who is not so bright at all. And yes, I believe I disappointed my dad, but I believe he is beginning to feel more proud. I will tell you one thing. I could have been better than this. Had I come to this country single, or younger, I could have been better, and I would not have been sitting down here with you at this level.

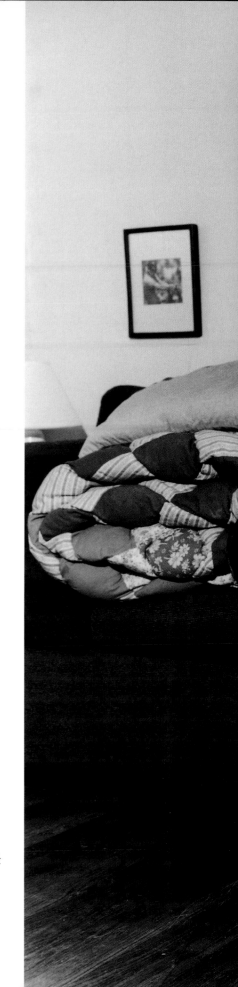

Gary Newmark

Gary Newmark
Loading Dock Shipper/Receiver, Harvard Coop

You want to know about regular working stiffs? You want to know what I do? I unloaded from a truck probably every book you ever read at Harvard. That's what I do. And you want to know what kind of life I've lived for twenty-three years working in that place? Twenty-three years. It was nothing that I planned. It was nothing that I set for a goal. It was just, get a job, so I got a job.

Anyone can do my job. It takes no real skill. In three months someone could know what they're doing. See, no one stays at a job more than a year these days. I personally believe they design it so it's not worth it. I feel like they want me to leave. It's not even about personality and whether they like you or not; it's about saving money. And I cost them a lot of money. I cost them thirty-nine paid days off a year, four weeks' vacation, three personal days, six sick days, and a medical plan. It used to be a good thing to work for a company twenty-three years. Now it's like I'm a thorn in their side. They'd be happy to hire some kid, and that way they wouldn't have to pay his insurance or anything unless of course he decides to stay for more than six months. I feel like I have no choice. With my skills, which are none—and not to put myself down, because a lot of common people used to survive by just working these kinds of jobs—but in today's day and age, you just can't do that anymore.

All my friends left Cambridge because they can't afford it. After twenty-three years I make fifteen bucks an hour, and I work my second job too—selling papers and magazines in Harvard Square—so you'd think I'd be doing all right with that, but I've got to move too. Next month I'm moving to Arlington. You just can't afford it.

I started working here when I was eighteen. I'm forty-four now. I'm a picture of stability. But things have changed. Hard work, honesty, and reliability really don't stand for shit anymore. And those are three of the things I have. America's not designed that way anymore. It's designed like you work a few months, three months, five months, we terminate you, we hire you temporarily. It would be really, really stupid for me to quit—I'll never get four weeks' vacation again. Took me ten years to get that.

I grew up in Arlington. Arlington public high—regulation school, I was a regulation student. I passed. No one in my family was ever a student, except one cousin who's this and he's that, and he's very, very successful. Whether that makes him happy I don't know. I just know he's the only one in our family that went to an Ivy League school. Not me. I don't even know any of the professors here. I don't even have any concept of what they do for a profession.

I mean, an average all-American person can't survive. I mean, a regular person. I don't want to go back to making $5.25 an hour. The jobs out there are all either for really technical, highly skilled people, or they're really, really down in the bottom of the barrel, McDonald's jobs and CVS jobs. It just seems to be getting farther and farther apart now.

Working at this place—you were never going to get rich working here, but to be honest with you, who wants to be rich? Those people are miserable too. People are people, you know what I mean? They got the same headaches, they got the same problems at home. It's funny the way America is. But you know, it's good to talk about this. It's like I matter. Someone once asked me, "Don't you have any career goals?" I go, "No, not really." So she goes, "So why are you working?" And I go, "Why you think I'm working? To eat. To have a roof over my head. Why else do people work?"

OVERLEAF: *Edgar Barrios*

Amadeo Lopez, Custodian, Harvard Business School, 2:18 A.M.
(wearing coworker's shirt).

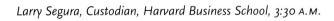

Larry Segura, Custodian, Harvard Business School, 3:30 A.M.

Phil LeBlanc, Custodian, Harvard Business School, 6:30 A.M.

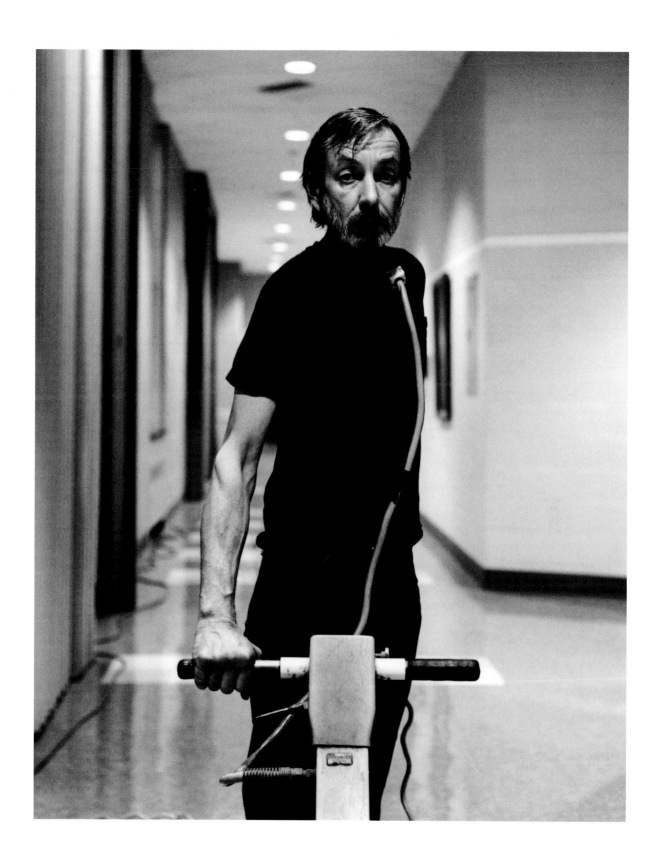

Success is a daily issue.
STREET JOURNA
Paper and Paperboard
LSU STOP TEXAS 5-4

Danny Meagher

Security Guard and Vice President, Harvard Security Guards' Union

There are things about Harvard that are really fine and beautiful things that are even noble. My wife got both her degrees from Harvard despite the fact that she didn't have no damn money. But she was smart and Harvard saw to it that she was able to come here and get an education based on the fact that she had the brain to do it, and that is a great thing. I love working in the museums, I love being around the art, but there are things about how the university views the working class that have never changed. In so many ways, they simply do not respect the rights, privileges, and dignities of the working class.

Over the past ten years, Harvard's hit our union with wage cuts, they've eliminated sick days, and they've outsourced ninety percent of the guard positions on campus. We had over a hundred and twenty guards in the union, and today we're down to about twenty. They busted our union and replaced us with lower-paid, nonunion guards. Do you think those guards are going to care more about this job, and take it seriously, if that's how seriously Harvard takes them? I take my job seriously. I am responsible for millions of dollars of artwork. I mean, if there's a heist at the museum and somebody comes in there with a sawed-off shotgun one day, it ain't gonna be the administrators, the director of the museum, or the head of security looking down the barrel of that shotgun. It's gonna be me or one of my coworkers. Plus, you've got to wonder, if you have some guy making a poor wage standing next to a painting that's worth seventy million dollars, and he's got a wife and kids at home who are eating macaroni and cheese, is that guy one day going to look at that painting and think, "Man, that painting's my ticket out of here"? Now, it's nothing I think about, or anyone I know for that matter, but at least in theory it is one reason you should pay people the value of their labor.

Personally, I'd like to have a staff ID with access to the gym and the libraries so that we could check books out to educate ourselves about the art we guard. I'm a photographer and a painter and I have educated myself at some expense about the art I guard by going to various used-book stores. I have a pretty large collection of art books at home. But to me, free access to the library seems like a fair request of a university. I mean, it's fairly often that I will look at the paintings with the students and help them understand them. They come in here for an assignment, and if you know how to explain an aspect of some painting that may seem very arcane to them, that's a good thing. Sometimes you have students trying to critically analyze a work of art that you've been looking at over and over again for two straight years. You see things in that painting that they're not going to find in ten minutes. And you point those things out to them and they may understand it better and get a better grade—and that's a good thing. That's the kind of relationship that's good to have with the student body.

And generally, I think the student body at Harvard has a better conscience and a more sophisticated social and political awareness than student bodies at a lot of other institutions. The state college I went to in Pennsylvania—I remember once seeing a bunch of students throwing snowballs at local coal miners who had gone on strike. I'm from Indiana County in western Pennsylvania and my grandfather started working in the coal mines when he was a kid. Everyone in Indiana County seemed to join the army or become a coal miner or worked in the steel mills. And I could see how those people built this country, how the infrastructure of this country was created out of the steel mills and coal mines of western Pennsylvania and West Virginia and eastern Kentucky. I sometimes think about my grandfather, working in the mines. And my life is very different from theirs, and my children's lives are even more different. But he and his coworkers fought really hard their whole lives, and one of the reasons life is better for me and my children is because they fought so hard. To give us a living wage with decent benefits, for example, would not break the university, and it would also satisfy the philosophical and moral principles that Harvard tells everybody they stand for.

Harvard constantly speaks of humanistic ideals and the truth and morals. I believe that Harvard is about those things, but when it comes to dealing with the workers in my union, those things are set aside for economic convenience. Those ideals are fundamentally important. I think anybody who went to this university would be really pissed off if they realized, "I learned these humane concepts and these philosophical and moral ideas, and how am I supposed to carry that forward as a person if certain administrators set aside all of those very profound moral ideas in order to squeeze the last drop of blood out of a group of low-wage workers?"

I didn't go to Harvard, but I was taught that if you are a man without honor then you are nothing. It's not what you do to the most powerful person, it is how you treat the least powerful people that determines whether you have honor. To have a moral view of your fellow man is not an empty concept to me. When I see people in a position of power treat powerless people with a disregard for their humanity, that is insulting and it is a scandal that reflects disrepute on the institution. The cost of living in this area is so high that the city of Cambridge now pays a minimum wage of eleven dollars an hour and is demanding that Harvard do the same, but Harvard insists on paying substantially less. The situation is a scandal. I just think Harvard's attitude toward its workers reflects badly on us all, and I think it also reflects badly on the students. It affects them, because they are getting an education that says it stands for a humanistic view when it has a policy of telling workers performing a very valuable service that they should work for nothing. Well the students learn that part, too, even though it's not taught explicitly in the classroom.

Udine Green, Custodian, William James Hall

Vinela Tejeda
Custodian, Vanderbilt Hall, Harvard Medical School

Those are my daughters. And that's in our apartment, in the Jamaica Plain projects. Diani is the oldest, Vanessa is in the middle, and Aurora is the youngest. My schedule is to get up very early, prepare breakfast, get Diani ready to get on the school bus, bring my other daughter to school, then drop Aurora off at my sister's. I get home tired. Tired from work. So I am happy to be home. I take off all my clothes and I bathe. Then I start cleaning, washing clothes, and I don't even feel like eating, because work, it gives me—well, seeing such things—I don't even feel like eating. But I have to prepare supper. Then Diani gets home. Then Vanessa gets home. And I always have appointments, things to do with the girls. If I have something to do with one of the girls I go with that girl and the others watch television. And that's it. That's how my time passes, and that's how all my days go.

I tell my daughters to study so that they will never work like I do. I have done this work for twelve years. My mom and dad, when I got to the U.S., they said for me not to do this kind of work. They said that I'd have a rough life and that it would be scary. But I told them I had to do it, and that I wouldn't do it so much for myself as for the girls.

My hope is in my children. I want for them to study and to learn the language well and prepare themselves—for another class of work. There will always be people cleaning the toilets at Harvard. But I want the best jobs for them. For myself, I cannot ask for anything very high up, realistically speaking. But I would love to work at least in a store. I worked as a cashier in my country. But in the very least I'd want a job less heavy. Maybe in a supermarket. The only thing I'm afraid of is my English, because the customer could ask something and I would not know what it is. But when you get the chance to come to this country, you go, and you may not have had the chance to learn English yet. And so here I am.

After high school, you see, I didn't want to go to college; only to come to the United States, to find a better future for me and my children. And so I came to the U.S. like everybody does—the unofficial way. And I came without my kids. I wanted to work in a bank because I liked accounting. But as I came here, I had to start work as soon as I came here because I had to save money to bring Diani here. And things here started getting more complicated because I didn't have papers, and I could not go to school and I had to work, and I had to keep cleaning. I couldn't get out of it.

I clean Vanderbilt Hall, where the medical students live. For the most part I clean rest rooms and kitchens. The hardest are the bathtubs, the showers, the stoves, everything in the kitchens. Sometimes the students leave pots and pans out in the kitchens for days, which can be difficult. But there are others that are really good people. With the students, I am as they wish. If they greet me, I greet them. And if they don't greet me, well I don't greet them either.

There are about seven of us, all women, who work here cleaning all six floors. I am not particularly proud of myself, but at least I always finish my work. I feel good about the fact that I complete my work. And thank God the supervisors have never had to call me in.

Mondays are the hardest days to clean because one finds everything strewn all over the place. The bathrooms are all wet with toilet paper, paper towels all over the place. The bathtub full of hairs, but one has to clean it. I put on my gloves and I protect myself. Where hundreds of students live, using the kitchen, using the bathroom, imagine how things get. There is also a ton of work to be done before the students come back from the summer. Every corner needs to be cleaned.

We have to protect ourselves when cleaning the rest rooms. We use gloves, and they give us good chemicals. I don't like that part but I do it. I do it because I need to. I don't know English well and I can't really apply at another job. So I have to do it. But it's okay, especially because I have a good supervisor, who is really great with us. He helps us and he doesn't pressure us too much.

I work seven days a week. I work eight hours on Saturdays and Sundays, doing the same job, in the same building, but it is for a different company. The problem with that is that I work two part-time jobs for two different companies, and so I do not qualify for health benefits with either one. I'd love to work one full-time job during the week, and to have benefits and weekends free to be with my daughters. But they say full time is not available right now. I don't like leaving the little ones home alone on the weekend. Because now when I leave, Diani, my oldest, stays there with the younger ones, or sometimes my sister will come stay with them. She doesn't have much of a home, my sister, so sometimes she'll spend the night too. We make room. Vanessa and Diani sleep together. I sleep with the little one. I like to be here at night to help them with homework and just to keep an eye on them.

I would like health benefits very much. Very much. I was absent two weeks once, because I was having an operation on a vein in my leg, and that week I didn't make any money because I couldn't work. When you take a leave to have a baby it's the same thing. Because I have no benefits. They give you two months to be at home but you aren't making any money.

When I had my daughters, I worked until I couldn't anymore. Past eight months. But I needed to, to save the money. They try to be considerate when you are pregnant, though. They give you lighter work and they try to get someone else to clean the bathtubs for you, because if you slip that can be dangerous. Now after the Living Wage Campaign, at least they've given us a raise to eleven dollars and thirty-five cents. It's better, but I'm still only at a hundred and sixty-two dollars a week, after taxes—six hundred and forty-eight dollars a month.

When I am working, I think at times about how I feel uncomfortable with this life here. "Always the same," I think, "always the same." But then I calm down because I realize I just have to work. I have three daughters, I have to support them. At other times I think of taking off for my country. And again I tell myself, "I'd better not. Now my girls are studying here. Now they speak English. I am obliged to stay." I feel trapped sometimes. Or I feel it's an embarrassment to be working in bathrooms and all. Or it makes me feel embarrassment or shame around the students, because at times they're not considerate when they make a mess in the bathrooms. And I will have to clean that up. Sometimes I think I made a bad decision in wanting to come to the United States. But at the same time, I think I have also acquired many things. I had two of my daughters here. And I am now legal here in this country; I have acquired my citizenship. And at least I work, although it's not a great job. At least I have my apartment. At least I have a roof. I don't have money but at least I live tranquilly. Having children has held me back, but I do not feel bad about that because they will move on. I would like us to move on together, maybe move back to Santo Domingo. Build a nice house there, for me and my daughters to live in comfortably and peacefully.

Martha Eshetu, Line Server, Lowell House

Kevin Reeves, Dishwasher, Lowell House

Reinaldo Macharo, Custodian, Lamont Library

Steve McComb, President, Harvard Security Guards' Union

Frank Morley
Custodian, Littauer Center for Public Administration

I recently had to go into an office and the professor was in there, and he's got the problem written on the board, and he's sitting there studying that thing, and I'm standing there fixing the file cabinet. The drawers were jamming, and the man didn't even flinch. I swear, the man didn't even know I was there. About twenty minutes later, he asked me if I fixed his cabinet yet. I told him I finished it twenty minutes ago. You might initially think it's a class thing, but it's not that at all. It's just they're so busy, and in a way, I've always admired a person who can sit down and be totally riveted right on whatever they're doing.

I'm the only one who cleans this building during the day and I got ninety-four rooms here. Once, between my two jobs I worked thirty-five days straight without a day off. I can usually pull that off, but this week, for example, I'm starting to catch a cold. A lot of us are tired. Tired of watching every dime, too. But it's like everyone's afraid to speak up. Most of the people who work for UNICCO come from other countries, primarily Spanish-speaking countries, because they're here on a green card there's intimidation going on. You hear stories that managers threaten to call the immigration office if they ask for a raise or if they ask for their vacation time. And if you lose your job with a green card, you have thirty days to get a new job or you're out of the country. One guy didn't get paid time and a half for his overtime, but the guy was so scared he wouldn't say anything. Once I requested a vacation and forty-five minutes later two supervisors came over and said, "What do you mean, you're taking a vacation?" See, UNICCO advertises that you get vacation, but in reality it's a little different. All that, and we have a union, Local Two-fifty-four of SEIU—the Service Employees' International Union.

My alarm goes off at four in the morning. That morning time is the only real time I have to myself. I shower, I shave, I listen to the news. Out the door by five-thirty. Get to the station by five-fifty. Catch the train at five fifty-five. Get to work at seven fifteen. All told it's an hour and forty-five minutes from Mansfield. I finish working for Harvard at four P.M., get on the train, grab a cup of coffee, throw down a doughnut, get off the train, and walk—twenty minutes from the station to the supermarket. I bag and stock until ten-thirty P.M., walk back to the train, take it home, get in the door around eleven-thirty. In bed around midnight— usually I hit the pillow and I'm out. Up again by four A.M. I've been on that schedule for a little over two years now.

There are a lot of days when you're walking around in a fog. But you don't think on it too much—you just go. There was a time when I was working Monday to Friday and four hours Saturday and four hours Sunday. I stopped that, but for a while after that I was still waking up early Saturday mornings, thinking I was going to work, getting dressed, until halfway through it I realized I didn't have to. Now, Saturdays I'll clean up at home, grocery-shop, do laundry. Sundays I sit down and watch football. Time is precious—at least at age sixty-one it is.

Right now I'm using the retirement money to pay back the money I borrowed from the bank. So I still got some money in the retirement fund, but that'll be gone soon. Still, I'd like to go out and indulge a little, you know? Sit down at a place and eat. I do that now when I get the tax refund. Nowadays, I tend to eat at work when I can. After the luncheons, we get a shot at the leftovers. So you save money where you can.

You've got to remember with a cleaning company that their primary purpose is to make a profit. Managers always try to cut expenses, and they see wages as expenses. They forget that it's people—it's a person they're talking about who's trying to live on that. For example, they'll keep your hours down below seventeen a week so they don't have to pay you benefits. That's part of their cost control. It's just that I'm tired up here, in the head, and I'm tired physically. Things bug me that normally don't. Sometimes I just need to back off and cool down a little.

I've been wearing a custodial uniform now going on twenty years. And I think by now they figure they own me like a piece of equipment, like a barrel or a buffing machine. Plus, people figure if I had any brains, I'd be doing something else. But it's really got nothing to do with being lazy or not having the smarts. I work hard, and I did a few years for a while at Roxbury College. I got an associate's degree in management, and I was going for the bachelor's. I was going to start my own business. That's when my father was diagnosed with cancer. My mother too, eight months later, so I hung up the school.

We recently got a raise, though, after three years of the Living Wage Campaign, the sit-in, and then finally after nine of us went so far as to get arrested at a rally. That was big news. It was pretty soon after that that we won our contract. So now I'll go from ten dollars to about eleven-fifty. That buck-fifty adds up to twelve dollars a day, sixty dollars a week, which may not sound like a lot to some people, but in my case you don't sneeze at it. Ever since the sixties, we always looked to the college students to get the action going. They'd get out there and do the work and get people to get out on the streets. The students have the knowledge to do the organizing. And they don't have jobs to lose and families to feed, so they can take the risks, they can get out there when we can't.

Frank Morley, arrested at a custodians' rally. Frank, along with a number of students and union organizers, was arrested for blocking traffic on Massachusetts Avenue. They sat down in the middle of the street to protest Harvard's post–Living Wage sit-in wage offer. The university's offer was subsequently increased.

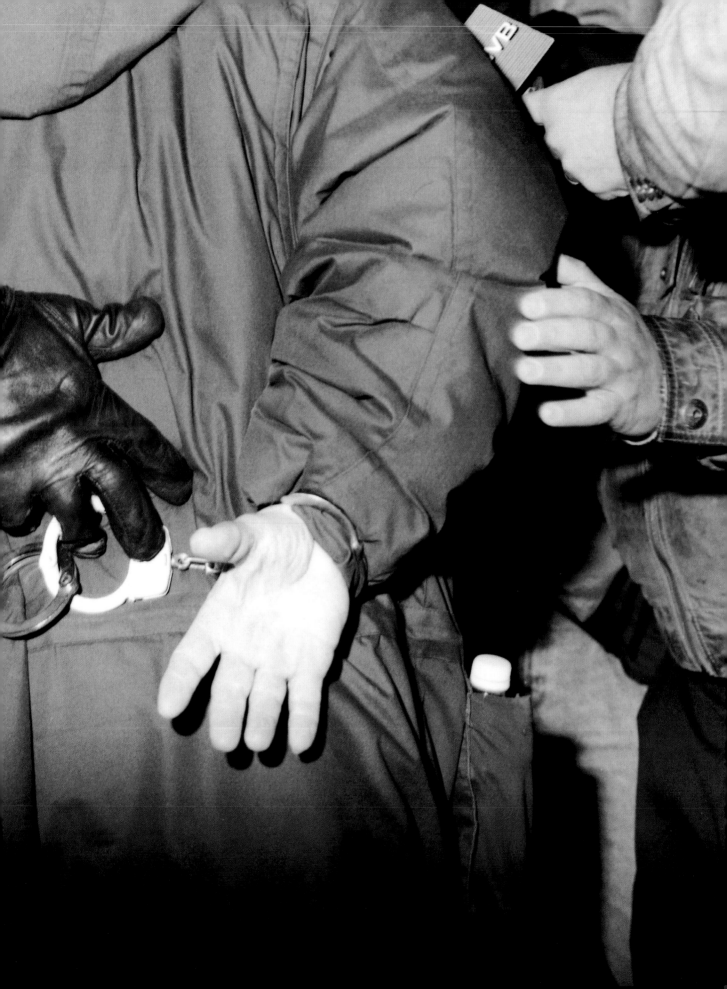

Appendix

The Narratives in Context

According to the Washington-based Economic Policy Institute, minimum-wage workers in most major American cities have to work nearly eighty hours a week just to cover their housing, food, and other basic living expenses.[1] Even the briefest conversation with service workers at Harvard made clear that workers needed new protections and that the 2002 federal minimum wage ($5.15 an hour) and the 2002 Massachusetts minimum wage ($6.75 an hour) were inadequate for an adult living in or near any major city.

In Massachusetts—already the third most expensive state in the United States in which to live[2]—workers' problems have been exacerbated by rising housing costs, especially after 1997, when Boston and Cambridge became the first major American cities since the 1950s to repeal their rent-control policies.[3] As rents rose, forcing workers out of the metropolitan area, public pressure prompted the city governments of Boston and Cambridge to pass their own living wage ordinances, as nearly a hundred other American cities have done since the mid-1990s. Though different cities have used different formulas, the exact living wage figure was always determined by calculating the hourly wage a local employee must earn (in a forty-hour week) to cover his or her housing, food, and other basic living costs.[4] The Cambridge ordinance—passed in 1999 at $10 per hour, now adjusted to $11.11 per hour—covered all workers hired directly by the city, including workers of private firms with significant city contracts. The idea of the Harvard Living Wage Campaign, then, was to put pressure on Harvard, the largest employer in Cambridge, to pay its workers the same living wage guaranteed by the city of Cambridge. Going one step beyond the city's standard, our campaign added that Harvard should provide every worker with affordable health benefits.

While Boston-area workers were struggling to keep up with the cost of living, Harvard service workers were dealt a crippling blow when top administrators at the university began cutting their wages, starting in the early 1990s and continuing through the rest of the decade. The most disturbing fact about these wage cuts (the details of which are below) is that they came at the very same time Harvard's wealth was growing at an unprecedented and exponential rate.

Between 1994 and 2001, Harvard's endowment nearly tripled from $7 billion to $20 billion,[5] distinguishing the university as the wealthiest nonprofit institution in the world with the exception of the Roman Catholic Church.[6] Were Harvard classified as a for-profit business, the sum would rank Harvard sixth on the Forbes 400 list.[7] The explosive growth of the endowment was fueled by a seven-year capital campaign that brought in, on average, $1 million per day from alumni between 1992 and 1999.[8] As money was raised, the Harvard Management Company—Harvard's investment firm—invested the money with historic success. Over that seven-year period, the endowment grew, on average, more than $5.5 million per day. In 1999, Harvard's most successful fiscal year, the endowment grew by $4.8 billion—an increase larger than the total endowments of the Massachusetts Institute of Technology ($4.3 billion), Columbia University ($3.6 billion), Dartmouth College ($1.7 billion), or Georgetown University ($745 million).[9] It should be noted that Harvard paid some of its employees quite well during this boom. In 2000, for example, Harvard's top five portfolio managers collectively earned more than $50 million in bonuses.[10] The university's top manager alone earned $17 million.[11]

Exactly what happened and how so much money was made in these years is still something of a mystery to those without inside knowledge, but it is an episode that demands the closest scrutiny by investigative reporters. The primary whistle-blower and investigator so far has been HarvardWatch, a student- and alumni-run organization designed to research Harvard's financial investments. A quick visit to HarvardWatch's Web site (www.harvardwatch.org) is enough to understand that the financial connections, friendships, and favors that fueled Harvard's financial boom are all but obvious. In recent years, HarvardWatch has focused much of its attention on the individual relationships of Harvard's top investors and bankers, who are formally connected through the Harvard Corporation, the self-appointing, seven-person governing body responsible for making Harvard's most important financial decisions. In recent years, one of the corporation's primary but unofficial functions has been the development of profitable friendships and networks. Every corporation member, for example, is a director (or board member) and major stockholder in at least one of America's most powerful financial institutions.

Perhaps most notoriously, one of the corporation's most recent members included Herbert "Pug" Winokur, director and chair of Enron's Finance Committee throughout that company's long history of corruption. It should be noted that before Winokur was forced to resign from the Harvard Corporation, the Harvard Management Company shortsold its considerable stock in Enron, earning an estimated $50 million when the company subsequently collapsed.[12] In an interesting twist, Winokur's vacated seat on the corporation was filled by Robert E. Rubin, former U.S. treasury secretary, co-chairman at Goldman Sachs, director of Ford Motor Company, and most notably, director and chairman of the Executive Committee at Citigroup. It has since emerged that Citigroup made at least one "secret oral agreement" with Enron to help create bogus accounting figures to hide the company's massive debt and thereby artificially inflate the company's stock value.[13] Rubin—reported by HarvardWatch to have earned $16 million in 2001 from his various directorships, and reported to possess an additional $29 million in stock options—remains unaffected by the scandal. Implicated as well in Enron's accounting fabrications is J.P. Morgan, a longtime director of which (1976–2000) is Hanna Gray, who sat on the Harvard Corporation with Enron's Winokur while J.P. Morgan was helping to hide Enron's debt.[14]

Harvard Corporation also includes, for example, James R. Houghton, director of MetLife and director and former chairman at ExxonMobil; D. Ronald Daniel, former managing partner at McKinsey & Company (1976–1988) and director of Tricon Global Restaurants (Taco Bell, Pizza Hut and KFC); and university president Lawrence Summers, former chief economist of the World Bank (1991–1993) and, like Rubin, former U.S. treasury secretary (1999–2001).

Although economists, investors, and reporters have tended to look the other way over the years, Harvard's recent investments raise enormous legal and ethical questions that ought to be more closely examined. The messages Harvard sends to its students and to the international academic community are articulated not only in its classrooms but in its dealings with the world at large. The second half of the 1990s was an era of corporate gluttony and corruption, and Harvard was not above it all. Whether the deals were illegal or not, the fact is that during this era of unparalleled wealth, Harvard cut the wages of its lowest-paid workers.

In the same years Harvard's endowment tripled, the percentage of Harvard's directly hired janitors earning less than $10 per hour quadrupled from 20 percent to 82 percent. At the same time, the university continued to outsource every position it could to some of the lowest-paying and most exploitative contractors in the Boston area. On average, Harvard paid its new workers 20 percent less than the directly hired workers they were hired to replace. Administrators then demanded that all the remaining in-house workers accept the same lesser wages and benefits. The janitors were forced to give Harvard devastating concessions or see their jobs outsourced. They were (and still are) being "tested"; meaning, for example, their supervisors hide pennies on the floor to see if the custodians find them and sweep them up. When they fail to do so, they are "written up" in a formal complaint to the union, and the case is used against them in the administrative push to outsource. Quite often, the newly hired workers were also denied essential health benefits, including sick days, vacation time, and paid maternity leave. Today, roughly 90 percent of Harvard's guards, 55 percent of its custodians, and 30 percent of its dining service workers have been outsourced.[15] These workers are, as Barbara Ehrenreich so succinctly puts it, "the major philanthropists of our society. They neglect their own children so that the children of others will be cared for; they live in substandard housing so that other homes will be shiny and perfect; they endure privation so that inflation will be low and stock prices will be high. To be a member of the working poor is to be an anonymous donor, a nameless benefactor, to everyone else."[16]

Unofficially (because companies will not admit it and because it is nearly impossible to prove) outsourced workers were also stripped of certain rights and freedoms. Though many workers in this book address the issue, a common consequence of this laissez-faire approach to low-wage work was that many workers' rightfully earned break time and vacation time were overlooked and "forgotten." Again, though it is impossible to prove, there was simply a greater sense of insecurity at outsourced work sites, especially at those that were also nonunion. At the worst sites, workers I had known and had become friends with would sometimes suddenly disappear. When I pursued the issue with managers, I'd invariably get a cryptic reply such as, "They're not with us any longer."

It was evident on countless occasions when I walked into an employee break room at an outsourced site and asked if anyone was interested in being a part of this book that I had severely escalated the tension and fear in the room. It was common for the collective response to be silence and averted eyes. On other occasions, workers at outsourced sites sometimes spread the word not to speak with me. Though it frustrated me, I respected and understood their actions, knowing that if they felt too scared to speak openly, they probably had reason to be. It was under these troubling circumstances, after years of falling wages and assaults on workers' dignity, that the Living Wage Campaign began its organizing efforts.

The Living Wage Campaign at Harvard

The Harvard Living Wage Campaign began in the fall of 1998 with a handful of students and ended in the spring of 2001 with a three-week sit-in and thousands of demonstrators outside

Jean Phane, Harvard Custodian, looking at
President Larry Summers at a meeting about wages.

the president's office. It was not until we sat-in that large numbers of people from the community came out to support us. Before that, gaining moderate supporters was a struggle, and simply building consensus in the community that a living wage was a sensible idea was a lot of work. Many students are taught to dismiss progressive economic ideas in Harvard's classrooms. Introduction to Economics—with more than a thousand students, easily the most popular class—is taught by Martin Feldstein, formerly Ronald Reagan's chief economic adviser and currently a director of J.P. Morgan. As the issue grew to engulf the campus, Feldstein argued in his classroom that living wage policies were problematic, essentially because they were not market-driven. Our reply was based on the argument that morals, not markets, ought to determine the economy's lowest wages. We also handed out the worker narratives collected in this book. The narratives were a way for moderates, who had not been swayed and may have been turned off by student activists, to identify with workers and to hear what they wanted.

We canvassed the student body over a period of years, using the narratives, fact sheets, op-eds, and lengthy reports to explain our arguments and debunk myths, such as "a living wage would lead to layoffs" or "if Harvard paid a living wage, it would have to raise tuition or abandon some of its financial aid." In response to these ideas, we publicized a study by the Economic Policy Institute, which showed that the increase in labor costs as a result of implementing a living wage was, for most firms, less than 2 percent of the firm's total production costs. We talked to other student organizations on campus and throughout Boston. In time, nearly a hundred such organizations came on board to support us. We organized a few big rallies each semester, and although we met with administrators just as often, two years passed without any significant sign that the administration was willing to address the problem. We resorted to increasingly creative and aggressive tactics to put pressure on the university. Aside from big rallies to demonstrate numbers, we held targeted actions to pressure important decision makers. For example, when the Harvard Corporation board members denied our request for a meeting, we went to members' individual offices and homes in New York City. We staged "teach-ins" in the offices of administrators to educate them about workers' lives and the need for a living wage. We crashed the president's Christmas party, sang him a "living-wage carol," and read aloud workers' narratives.

We targeted Harvard when it was vulnerable—preempting the official speeches with our own at junior parents' weekend, demonstrating outside Larry Summers's press conference when his appointment was announced, and organizing rallies when the prospective freshman class visited. We convinced Harvard alumni to sign cards pledging not to donate to Harvard until it passed a living wage policy. We used the media and Harvard's name to shed light on the lives of its workers and to put public pressure on the administration. We created events to catch media attention and brought in celebrity speakers, such as Matt Damon and Ben Affleck. As for worker involvement, at the beginning there was only a small core of workers who felt they had the security and support to speak publicly and come to demonstrations. Danny Meagher and Frank Morley, both of whom are in this book, were two of the early activists, though many more people would become visible as the months passed. Occasionally, larger numbers of workers would turn out, but it took years before workers came out in meaningful numbers and ultimately felt safe being seen at rallies and speaking in public. As is clear from a number of the narratives, workers were discouraged from participating, because managerial intimidation was so common. The campaign had been student-initiated as well, so it took a long time to build an effective, healthy partnership with the workers. As the campaign grew in numbers and in popularity, and especially after the sit-in, workers did become increasingly confident speaking out in public. Every campus union was at least technically on board, though some were more complacent and hesitant than others.

As pressure built, Harvard tried to smother the issue. The administration formed a committee of professors to examine the idea of a living wage. Many of the professors had distinctly conservative tendencies, and for the six or more months while they deliberated, Harvard declared the issue closed. Finally, the committee suggested that Harvard offer an increased number of free English classes for its workers, but to our disappointment this suggestion went no further. We were discouraged, but driven to push harder, especially because by then it seemed that the majority of students on campus supported us. Years of talking to people had built a consensus on the issue, and though most of our supporters were not "activists," a large number of people had done at least something for the campaign, for example, attending an event, asking a professor to sign a petition, or writing a letter to the dean. All in all, we had organized more than twenty large public rallies and had sat through just as many fruitless meetings with various administrators.

Despite our increasingly broad-based support, a number of students soon stopped showing up at meetings, discouraged by our failure to make any concrete progress with the administration. It appeared that Harvard was content to wait us out. Eventually, they correctly figured, we'd have to graduate.

The Sit-in

In January 2001, more than three years after the first living wage meeting, we made a tentative decision to sit in by the end of the school year if the administration had still not seriously addressed the issue. We had always considered a sit-in a last-ditch option, and one that could easily backfire. Not only would escalation to that degree turn off some of our more moderate supporters but, if it somehow failed, it would be an embarrassing setback to the campaign. But by April it seemed we had exhausted our options, and we understood that unless public pressure forced them to, the administration was not going to move.

On April 18, fifty of us (mostly students and a handful of alumni) stormed into Massachusetts Hall, which houses the office of the university's president. We had anticipated a three-day stay, though we would remain for three weeks. At least fifty students remained outside to coordinate support and contact members of the media, whom we saw not only as potential

Harvard Police (in plain clothes) filming workers at rally.

supporters but as a set of eyes for protection. In 1968, when two hundred Harvard students took over another administration building in protest of Harvard's collaboration with ROTC, the doors were smashed down and the students were dragged out and beaten by more than four hundred policemen who had been called in at the administration's orders. Harvard was taught a humiliating lesson the next day, though, when the *New York Times* prominently ran a photograph of a student whose face was covered in blood, his skull smashed.[17] Our strategy was to give Harvard a choice: Either they could make significant concessions on the wage issue or they could arrest their own students with the news cameras recording the results.

Support came slowly at first. As we had predicted, some students were shocked by the escalation in our tactics. The student government and the *Harvard Crimson* officially condemned our methods of protest. The first few days were painful. Few people came to support us and no media covered the story. We suspected higher-ups at Harvard had put pressure on their media contacts to downplay the event. Still, we worked hard from the inside. Nearly all of us had borrowed or bought cell phones going in, and a number of us had brought laptops and had connected to the Internet by phone lines in the building. We contacted students, workers, and community members. We pinpointed key, influential individuals and asked them to support the sit-in however they could. We called and e-mailed every possible press contact, professor, and politician. We worked feverishly, using the drama and urgency of the sit-in to recruit as many supporters as possible. People on the fence were forced to take sides, and the majority of people seemed to be siding with the workers.

Because there were on average ten to twenty cops in and around the building each night, we took turns staying awake. We got to know the cops well, and with time a few of them befriended us and would even talk quietly of their support for us and their sense of solidarity with the rest of the workers. Although initially they had refused to let food in the building, they quickly realized that preventing food from coming in would inadvertently force us into a hunger strike—a tactic few of us wanted to employ, but one the administration wanted even less, as it would have escalated the drama and caused a media frenzy. When a dozen dining service workers showed up with pizzas and wearing living wage buttons, they said they had a responsibility to feed their students. The cops were forced to open the doors. Dining workers continued happily to deliver food, starting the day with gallon jugs of coffee and returning for lunch and dinner. A few days later, the dining workers voted unanimously and in solidarity with the campaign for a strike authorization, thereby empowering their union representatives to call a strike at any moment. In an inspiring and impromptu celebration after the vote, the three hundred dining workers who attended the vote surrounded Massachusetts Hall and took over the streets outside the building, dancing and chanting with megaphones. It was a display of pride and strength and an outpouring of emotion unlike any we had seen. We, too, danced through the building, our adrenaline pumping, clapping and chanting back at them. The event was an inspiration to other workers as well, and an increasing number of them began to show up at the sit-in on their lunch breaks and after work. Custodians began organizing their own demonstrations and giving interviews, often freely giving their own names as well. Workers who had not yet been involved began to speak out and spend a lot of time around the sit-in. For some, the highly public expression of power and pride was a new and thrilling experience.

After a week, hundreds of supporters were rallying outside every day. The crowds consisted mostly of students, though some professors and other workers and a variety of people from the Boston community had come out as well. People began sleeping out in Harvard Yard, and soon nearly a hundred tents sprang up outside Massachusetts Hall. Senators Ted Kennedy and John Kerry visited the sit-in, along with AFL-CIO president John Sweeney and former secretary of labor Robert Reich. A core group of committed faculty members managed to secure a statement of support from a majority of faculty. The press coverage grew increasingly dramatic and supportive. All the national television networks began covering the story, and Bob Herbert twice wrote articles backing us on the op-ed pages of the *New York Times,* one of which went so far as to call us "heroes."[18]

The scene around Massachusetts Hall had become something of a circus. Hundreds of people were milling around a massive "tent city," posters and papers were strewn everywhere, and there were speeches, live music, dance performances, and a constant stream of reporters. It was the most uninhibited and hopeful we had ever seen the Harvard community. The media seemed to love it, fixating on the bizarre juxtaposition of chaos in the customarily immaculate Harvard Yard. Though we were grateful for the coverage we could get, some reporters were more interested in the carnival-like atmosphere than in the issues. Reporters tried to peek in windows to ask whether we were doing our homework and what it was like to "shower" in the sink (all we had was a sink and toilet for the fifty of us). It was completely unexpected and highly unusual for a student protest to get such coverage. We only hoped the coverage would embarrass and pressure the Harvard administration, as well as inspire living wage campaigns on other campuses. Since the sit-in, in fact, students on more than two dozen college campuses have started their own living wage campaigns.

Despite the increased pressure, after two weeks of sitting-in, the administration still refused to meet with us. The support outside had begun to plateau; President Rudenstine had addressed us only once, saying he would resign before "giving in." It appeared we were approaching a stalemate, one we would eventually be forced to lose because we could not sit-in forever. The numbers on the inside had dwindled from fifty to thirty, and of those left, emotional and psychological burnout was imminent. Early spring had brought eighty- and ninety-degree temperatures, the effects of which were stifling inside Massachusetts Hall. Unable to shower or change our clothes, we were soon covered in a layer of grease, and the smell inside had caused more than one police officer to gag when he walked into the building. I myself had become increasingly depressed, claustrophobic, and generally cynical about the sit-in's prospects. Some of us worked incessantly, others could do nothing but sleep and read all day, knowing that, if nothing else, their stubborn, if idle, presence in the building was holding some of the public's interest and keeping the pressure on the university.

It was at this uncertain stage that my friend Aaron Bartley was able to convince John Hiatt, the AFL-CIO's top lawyer, to act as our representative. It was a remarkable development that boosted our spirits, and though Harvard had vowed never to negotiate with us, they agreed to negotiate with Hiatt in private regarding our demands.

Through Hiatt, Harvard offered the campaign a new committee, which the campaign itself would be able to help create. It seemed clear from the amount of public pressure that Harvard would have to offer significant concessions to its workers, though they refused to appear as having given in under such public scrutiny. They insisted on "due process," and though we were skeptical, Hiatt seemed to have been assured by higher-ups that the committee would lead to improvements for workers. He interpreted the committee as a face-saving measure, one that allowed the university to make concessions without appearing to have given in. We focused on influencing the committee's makeup and succeeded in getting two campaign members as well as two workers (Ed Childs, a dining employee, and Jean Phane, a custodian) on the committee. Both were union representatives and powerful speakers. Their presence on the committee was an important victory. They were likable and influential, and it would be difficult for any professor of economics to look either of them in the eye and say they did not deserve a living wage. The faculty on the committee was moderate but more progressive than those on the previous committee. As was fitting with the drama of the previous three weeks, a crowd of more than two thousand was waiting as the twenty-five remaining campaign members left the building.

In December 2001, after six months of research and meetings, the committee released its findings and recommendations.[19] To our disappointment, the committee members rejected the idea of a living wage, or any permanent wage floor, though they did make two key recommendations that the university adopted. Each would make a significant difference in the lives of workers on campus. The committee recommended a one-time wage increase to $11.35 per hour for all of the lowest-paid workers on campus; and in addition they implemented a formal "parity" policy that would prohibit Harvard from paying outsourced workers any less than directly hired workers. Although the wage rates are not guaranteed to rise with inflation or with the cost of living (that would require a living wage policy), the parity policy is a lasting victory for workers at Harvard. It is estimated that, as a result of the sit-in, approximately $3,738,000 is now redistributed annually by Harvard to more than a thousand of its lowest-paid workers.

Resolution

After a tumultuous, three-year campaign, there is now substantial worker-initiated organizing taking place at Harvard, mostly through the Harvard Workers' Center, which, unlike the Living Wage Campaign, was created jointly by students and workers. The custodial union, SEIU Local 254, continues to reorganize itself and is beginning to take a much more aggressive approach to its politics, and HarvardWatch is keeping an eye on Harvard's more questionable investments. There have been effects beyond Harvard as well. The city of Boston has raised its living wage standard in response to the sit-in and the ensuing media coverage; dozens of campuses have since started living wage campaigns; and a number of universities have changed their pay scales.

Despite the victories, the literal and psychological defeat of losing the battle for an actual living wage was significant. Symbolically, the point of a living wage is to acknowledge that the lives and well-being of the lowest-paid workers ought to be respected and defended, not treated merely as expenses. Practically speaking, the point of a living wage is to guarantee a decent wage and a healthy standard of living with regard to inflation and rising living costs, as well as to eliminate the need for a massive campaign every time those costs rise.

Yet even with a living wage, lasting progress still depends on our awareness of one another's working conditions. I hope that the narratives in this book positively affect our consciousness, and that the photographs affect the way we see.

Notes

1. See the Economic Policy Institute at www.epinet.org for details.
2. "Pricey Rents Put Massachusetts Among Nation's Most Expensive," The Associated Press State & Local Wire, October 2, 2001, *Business News;* and "High Costs Curb States' Job Growth," by Charles Stein, *The Boston Globe,* April 14, 1994, p. 73.
3. Tucker, William. The Cato Institute. "How Rent Control Drives Out Affordable Housing—Cato Policy Analysis No. 274." May 21, 1997.
4. In a 1999 recommendation to the City of Boston by the Washington-based Economic Policy Institute, the following monthly costs were calculated: Housing ($906), Food ($510), child care ($916), transportation ($221), health care ($387), other necessities ($439), and taxes ($703). The statistics are based on total monthly costs for a family of two working parents and two children. The numbers result in a living wage recommendation of $13.47/hour. As Barbara Ehrenreich points out in *Nickel and Dimed,* although the budget includes such "luxuries" as health insurance, a telephone and child care at a licensed center, it does not, for example, include meals at a restaurant, video rentals, Internet access, wine and liquor, or "even very much meat.".
5. "The Financial Facts." *Harvard Magazine,* January–February, 1997.
6. Berkman, Johanna. "Harvard's Hoard." *New York Times,* 24 June 2001, 39.
7. Berkman, Johanna. "Harvard's Hoard." *New York Times,* 24 June 2001, 39.
8. Jeffrey Tanenhaus, University Wire October 13, 1999.
9. Harvard Endowment Zooms a Third to $19.2 Billion, David Abel, Boston Globe, September 23, 2000 & Berkman, Johanna. "Harvard's Hoard." *New York Times,* 24 June 2001, 39.
10. Berkman, Johanna. "Harvard's Hoard." *New York Times,* 24 June 2001, 39.
11. Berkman, Johanna. "Harvard's Hoard." *New York Times,* 24 June 2001, 39.
12. Healy, Beth and Abel, David. "Harvard Students Say School May Have Profited by Fund's Short Selling of Enron," *The Boston Globe,* 1 February 2002. The exact amount made by Harvard is still unknown, although HarvardWatch estimates the university's profit to be in the range of $50 million. Details of this stock sale and the Harvard-Enron connections are available at www.harvardwatch.org.
13. Oppel, Richard Jr. and Eichenwald, Kurt. "Citigroup Said to Mold Deal to Help Enron Skirt Rules." *The New York Times,* 23 July 2002.
14. Gordon, Marcy, A. P. "Banks Sometimes Aware that Enron Used Deceptive Accounting, Senate Investigator Says." *The New York Times,* 23 July 2002.
15. "Outsourcing, its Discontents, and Some Solutions, A Report Prepared for HCECP by the Harvard Worker's Center." www.harvardwatch.org, www.hcs.harvard.edu/~pslm/livingwage, 12 October 2001, 1.
16. Ehrenreich, Barbara. *Nickel and Dimed.* New York: Metropolitan Books, 2001, 221.
17. Trumpbour, John. *How Harvard Rules,* Boston: South End Press, 1989, 390.
18. Herbert, Bob. "Harvard's Heroes." *The New York Times,* 3 May 2001, "op-ed" page; and Herbert, Bob. "Disparities at Harvard." *The New York Times,* 30 April 2001, "op-ed" page.
19. Its findings, which are available to the public at www.hcecp.harvard.edu, also include careful research about Harvard's recent history of outsourcing and wage-cutting.

Jimmy Joseph and Jovon Mcqueen

PAGES 160–161: *Running into Massachusetts Hall. The beginning of the sit-in.*

Management's negotiating team

Custodians' negotiating team

Reginald Boger and
James Roland, Sous Chefs,
Harvard Law School

Harvard Works Because We Do
Greg Halpern

Photographs and text © 2003 by Greg Halpern

Design by Laura Lindgren
The text of this book is set in Scala Sans, and the display type in Heliotype.

Manufactured by Mondadori Printing, Verona

Library of Congress Cataloging-in-Publication Data
Halpern, Greg.
  Harvard works because we do / photographs
and interviews by Greg Halpern ; foreword by
Studs Terkel.— 1st ed.
    p.   cm.
  ISBN 0-9714548-9-2
  1. Harvard University—Employees—Interviews.
2. Wages—College employees—Massachusetts—
Cambridge—History. 3. Harvard University—
Pictorial works. I. Title.
  LD2120.H35 2003
  378.744'4—dc21   2003013364

The author wishes to thank Aaron Bartley, the California College of Arts and Crafts, Tammy-Rae Carland, Sue Ciriclio, Robert Coles, Trevor Cox, Marjorie Garber, Paul Gellert, Jim Goldberg, Stephen Goldstine, Jaker Halpern, Stephen Halpern, Tammy Halpern, the Harvard Living Wage Campaign, the Harvard Union of Clerical and Technical Workers, Jim Hart, Todd Hido, Tisha Hooks, Chris Johnson, Artemis Joukowsky, Vicki Kennedy, Chris Killip, the LEF Foundation, Laura Lindgren, Kasia Lipska, Jim Mairs, John Merrill, Abner Nolan, Joe Regal, Beverly Sanford, Juliet Schor, Ian Simmons, Sage Sohier, Betty Stanton, Larry Sultan, Brooks Tompson, the Vermont Studio Center, Brook Wilensky-Lanford, Howard Zinn, and Paul Zuydhoek.

THE QUANTUCK LANE PRESS
Distributed by
W. W. Norton & Company, Inc.
500 Fifth Avenue, New York, NY 10110

W. W. Norton & Company Ltd.
Castle House, 75/76 Wells Street, London W1T 3QT

1 2 3 4 5 6 7 8 9 0